THE CBT SOCIAL ANXIETY WORKBOOK FOR WOMEN

ESSENTIAL COGNITIVE BEHAVIORAL SKILLS AND
TECHNIQUES TO OVERCOME FEAR AND ANXIOUS
BEHAVIOR, IMPROVE CONFIDENCE, AND FEEL
COMFORTABLE IN ANY SITUATION

ADELE PAYNE

CONTENTS

Your Free Gift

As a way of saying thanks for your purchase, I'm offering the book 7 Ways Anxiety Might Be Slowly Eating Away Your Life for FREE to my readers.

To get instant access just go to:

Inside the book, you will discover:

- Symptoms of anxiety
- Strategies that work for dealing with anxiety
- Overcoming your fear
- Building self-esteem and confidence

If you want to conquer your anxiety and become a social butterfly, make sure to grab the free book.

INTRODUCTION

Self-consciousness is the enemy of all art, be it acting, writing, painting, or living itself, which is the greatest art of all.

— RAY BRADBURY

As someone who had just become a teenager, I was not very fond of keeping up with trends and wearing clothes that most of my peers wore. In fact, my wardrobe was so limited that I would only replace my clothes if most of my old ones became torn or absolutely unfit for wearing anymore. You might think that I was admirably frugal or that I believed in sustainable fashion. Neither of these is the truth. It was an extreme act of self-preservation. You see, my body and mind reacted in weird ways whenever I had to go out in public. It didn't matter if I was going to an amazing restaurant, running an errand, or meeting my friends.

Once a certain plan was finalized, my body would become alert as if anticipating trauma or revisiting it. For hours before the event, my stomach would be upset, I'd get the chills, and be unable to move. Needless to say, this was exceptionally perplexing to my parents, who didn't understand why a seemingly fun event was making me behave this way. When you added an element of judgment to these events, my anxiety went through the roof. For example, if we had to go shopping, I would be thinking of the numerous salespeople in the store judging me for buying clothes that weren't meant for me or the mirrors in the trial room reflecting my insecurities back to me. My rational mind knew that no one cared *that* much about how I looked or what I wore, but my anxiety dismissed all reason.

When I thought I had handled everything my social anxiety could throw at me—mostly by staying home and avoiding every interaction possible—fate started getting creative with my life. A teacher I greatly admired decided that I would do well as a public speaker. Not only that, but they thought that my talents would shine brightest when I was made to take the stage without preparation—for example, through extempore speaking events. As you can imagine, this plan failed spectacularly in its first few attempts. I would be rooted to the ground—unable to open my mouth—as I stared silently at an audience of uncomfortable and pitying classmates staring back at me. Not surprisingly, my favorite teacher slowly became someone I resented and avoided as much as I could. Try as I might, I couldn't understand why they would insist on putting me—and others—through this torture on a regular basis.

One day, however, things took a turn. My teacher gave me a topic that I was passionate about, and by that time, I'd bombed on the stage so many times that I was beginning to get bored of it. Something else was happening at the time. Everyone that I'd been afraid of, all my worst scenarios—everything had already come to pass. I'd been laughed at, pitied, and dismissed by everyone who knew me. I'd frozen on the stage and felt like ages had passed me by before I could recover. In a weird way, no one cared about me anymore—not even my failures.

That day, all I wanted to do was talk about the topic presented to me. It wasn't that my anxiety vanished completely but that it became irrelevant to me. When I finished my speech that day, I was met by applause so thunderous that it drowned out even the now-meek voice of my inner critic. Later, I thought about how much I enjoyed the applause, but there was something else I enjoyed even more. After my speech, I had so many people come up to me to tell me how moved they were by what I had to say and how inspired they were when they heard me. I had never thought that the young girl who ran a fever at the thought of talking to a stranger could inspire so many people she barely knew.

That was the day I decided to work on my social anxiety in earnest and to make connections with new people as often as I could. The stronger these connections became, the more I realized what my social anxiety had been doing to me. What I had seen as protection for most of my life was actually a restriction. I had become the biggest barrier to my achievement of a rich and meaningful life. My carefully built "cocoon" had chained me to an existence that I didn't even want.

My past experiences laid the foundation for my current life as a coach and author who loves helping people overcome confidence and anxiety-related issues in their lives. As an adult, I've spent years trying to understand how social anxiety works and what makes it so difficult for people to overcome. The strategies I've written about in this book have helped many people—

including me—in overcoming their social anxiety and living a full life. Not everyone gets lucky with an amazing teacher like I did, but I'm hoping this book can act as the guide and mentor you need to become the best version of yourself.

This book is for anyone who feels like a social scenario is an invitation to judgment, criticism, and ridicule. This is for young girls and women who struggle with seeing their value in society and who feel like they need to dim their light or become small in order to live peacefully. This is for women who have repressed their traumas and haven't dealt with them, thus leading to low self-esteem.

If you think that you'll never escape the constant negative self-talk that goes on inside your head, this book will help you see things differently. There are three main parts to this book. In the first part, we'll learn about how social anxiety manifests in women and what the reasons are behind it. In the second part, we'll focus on cognitive behavioral therapy (CBT) as a tool for overcoming social anxiety and also discuss other methods of overcoming fear and anxiety in social situations. The last part will deal with building confidence and learning numerous skills to navigate social situations.

After reading this book, you should have the skills and techniques needed to process any past traumas around social situations, identify your triggers and negative thought patterns, and gradually gain the confidence to address your social anxiety and become a part of social scenarios that you tend to avoid.

Ultimately, the aim is to not only connect with others but also connect with yourself in a loving, respectful, and meaningful way. This book should help you see your presence as a gift to others—to see yourself as someone who enriches other people's lives simply by being a part of them. Let's take the first step toward the rest of your amazing life.

1

UNDERSTANDING SOCIAL ANXIETY

I f you've ever suffered from any mental health issue, chances are, you've often felt lonely. In some cases, you might have a supportive group of people around you. In others, you might struggle to get the help you need. In both cases, however, you might sometimes feel like you're the only one going through these issues. What's more, most of us get into the habit of blaming ourselves for how we're feeling. Not only does this make us feel lonelier, but it also exacerbates the very symptoms that we're trying to avoid.

In the chapter, we'll try to understand general anxiety as well as social anxiety in some detail. When we understand the causes and symptoms of these conditions, we'll feel less anxious about anxiety. This self-awareness is the first step toward managing our social anxiety.

UNDERSTANDING ANXIETY

The first thing to understand about anxiety is that everyone experiences it. To be human is to feel anxious every now and then, especially when the world stops making sense to us. This is why so many of us have become more anxious after the pandemic because the world has become extremely uncertain and scary. However, there's a difference between experiencing anxiety and being anxious, especially in the way that it affects your daily life. When the feelings of anxiety don't subside for a long time, and when they begin to interfere with your daily routines, you might be suffering from an anxiety disorder. If you find yourself overreacting to situations, or if you aren't able to control how you respond to unplanned scenarios, your anxiety might have gotten out of hand.

When you feel anxious, you're excessively worried about the present or future. This worry leads to extreme stress—which can manifest in physical, mental, and physiological ways.

For example, some of the most common symptoms of anxiety are

- trembling or twitching,
- excessive sweating,
- light-headedness,
- increased heart rate,
- irritability or mood swings,
- dealing with intrusive thoughts,
- nausea,
- diarrhea or frequent urination,
- frequent headaches,
- insomnia, and
- feelings of constant dread or apprehension.

Depending on how your anxiety manifests, you can experience different symptoms as well.

Another thing to understand about anxiety is that it might look like fear but is distinct from it. We generally feel fear when faced with a specific threat that is known to us. This threat could be real or imaginary, but you know what it is. Anxiety, on the other hand, is mostly related to uncertainty regarding the future. You might have some idea why you're anxious but it's not usually clear or specific. For example, when we have social anxiety, we're worried about whether we can take part in social scenarios and handle conversations with ease.

However, we don't know exactly what could go wrong. In fact, we don't even know *if* anything will go wrong. All we know is that we feel anxious about a number of unknowns that can make our lives more difficult. Fear usually resolves within a short period of time, but anxiety can go on—or feels like it's going on—forever.

The less we know about a situation, the more we tend to feel anxious about it. As you can see, this is a problem because we barely know enough about anything in our lives. Even so, some people are better equipped to handle anxiety than others.

What Causes Anxiety?

There are many factors that increase our chances of developing anxiety disorders. Let's go through some of them:

- **Genetics**—There's a chance that an anxious parent might pass on certain genes that might make their children predisposed toward anxiety disorders.
- **Environment**—The environment in which we grow up and the people we surround ourselves with might also play a role in developing anxiety. According to a study, babies whose mothers suffered from anxiety had a tendency to focus on situations that might lead to anxiety

(Morales et al., 2017). So, it's a combination of both genes and learned behaviors that can contribute toward anxiety disorders.

- **Exposure to trauma**—There are two main ways in which trauma can affect us. If we've been through a traumatic experience, we might develop general anxiety or anxiety related to that particular event. On the other hand, if we see or read about traumatic things happening to other people around us or in the media, we might develop anxiety through vicarious conditioning.

- **Stress**—When we're extremely stressed, it has an effect on our physical and mental health. This can also lead to anxiety if it goes unchecked. Chronic stress can make us feel like everything's out of control, which can exacerbate anxiety symptoms.

- **Physical ailments**—Certain physical ailments —such as heart arrhythmias—can also make us predisposed to anxiety issues.

- **Drug use**—Drug or alcohol addiction, as well as the withdrawal symptoms that come with quitting them, can lead to exacerbation of anxiety symptoms.

- **Brain injury**—Certain areas of our brain are responsible for the regulation of our emotions, as well as for how we react to stress and anxiety. When these areas are affected—either due to injury or illness—it can also affect our chances of developing anxiety disorders. This is also why extremely traumatic events can lead to anxiety disorders even if you weren't previously anxious.

- **Unease around new situations**—Also known as behavioral inhibition, this is a tendency to either feel extreme stress or fear in new situations or to completely withdraw when faced with unfamiliar people or situations. Most of us feel apprehensive when faced with such scenarios, but if you actively avoid them or panic at the thought of them—you might be experiencing social anxiety.

- **Focus on negative emotions**—All of us experience negative emotions from time to time. However, some of us might be more prone to experiencing emotions like guilt, sadness, fear, anxiety, and distress. In many cases, this is coupled with anxiety sensitivity, which means that we feel guilty about feeling anxious. In other words, if we've been conditioned to think that anxiety is a bad state of mind or that we should avoid it at all costs, there's a good chance that we might develop an anxiety disorder.

DIFFERENT TYPES OF ANXIETY

The Diagnostic and Statistical Manual of Mental Disorders: 5th edition, text revision (DSM-5-TR) identifies the following as anxiety disorders (Felman, 2023).

Generalized Anxiety Disorder

Generalized anxiety disorder (GAD) is a condition in which people worry too much and too often about unspecified things in their life. People who suffer from GAD experience many symptoms of anxiety—such as intrusive thoughts, fears about making the "wrong" decision regarding the future, inability to concentrate in the present, perpetually feeling tense, and trying to control everything by planning too much. However, they might not be able to pinpoint the actual reasons behind these symptoms. If a person has been dealing with these symptoms for six months or more, they're diagnosed with GAD by a doctor.

People with this disorder can sometimes exhibit heightened symptoms if they're ill or going through a period of extreme stress.

Panic Disorder

Sometimes, when we go through periods of heightened anxiety or stress, we might experience panic attacks. According to the Anxiety and Depression Association of America, we need to experience at least four of the following symptoms for it to be called a panic attack (Nall, 2023a):

- fear of death
- detachment from reality
- fear of losing our mind or losing control in general
- breathing difficulties or feeling like we're being choked
- feeling extremely hot or cold
- tightness in the chest or chest pain
- tingling sensation or numbness
- trembling, shaking, and/or sweating
- irregular heartbeat, rapid heart rate, or heart palpitations
- dizziness
- nausea and/or upset stomach

These attacks can occur due to certain triggers or because we're dealing with a lot of stress, but they can also occur without reason or warning. Depending on how frequent and severe your panic attacks are, a doctor might diagnose you as having a panic disorder.

Panic disorders can also be related to other anxiety and anxiety-adjacent disorders—such as obsessive-compulsive disorder (OCD), post-traumatic stress disorder (PTSD), generalized anxiety disorder (GAD), and agoraphobia.

Selective Mutism

Sometimes, children have difficulty talking or expressing themselves in front of people they're not comfortable around. This is different from an inability to speak that's physical or cognitive in nature. In these cases, the children are perfectly capable of speaking, they don't suffer from speech-related difficulties, and they might even have a great vocabulary and exceptional speaking skills. However, if they're anxious in certain settings, they might temporarily lose their ability to speak. For example, some kids are extremely chirpy at home but clam up when guests come over. Others might talk a lot among close friends but become extremely quiet in social situations. While this condition is more common in children, it can also affect adults. In many cases, selective mutism goes hand-in-hand with social anxiety disorder.

Phobias

Phobias are anxiety disorders that cause irrational and excessive fear related to a particular event, object, creature, or situation. These triggers can vary widely among people and they're usually very specific, meaning you can pinpoint the reason behind your phobia. In many cases, people are aware that their fears are exaggerated or that they aren't even real. However, this usually does nothing to reduce their anxiety, and they might spend most of their lives trying to actively avoid these triggers.

According to the American Psychiatric Association (APA), there are three types of phobias (Brazier, 2020):

- social phobia (also known as social anxiety)
- agoraphobia
- specific phobia

Social Anxiety Disorder (Social Phobia)

Almost everyone experiences a little bit of social anxiety every now and then. Some of us might feel nervous before an important event, or we might be apprehensive about talking in front of a large crowd. However, people who suffer from social anxiety disorder (SAD) experience extreme fear, embarrassment, or anxiety whenever they have to interact with people in social scenarios. This is different from being shy or introverted. We'll be discussing this condition in detail in the next section.

Agoraphobia

There's a common misconception when it comes to agoraphobia. Many people believe that this is a fear of open spaces but that's a restrictive view of this condition. In fact, people with this condition can be scared of any place or situation from which it might be difficult to escape if needed. This can include closed or confined spaces, crowded areas, or open and remote areas. Even places like elevators or public transport can trigger their anxiety. In extreme cases, such people don't even leave the house—because everything outside their house seems out of their control and risky. They might also worry about feeling embarrassed in situations where they're stuck and cannot ask for help from others. As mentioned before, panic disorders can also be related to agoraphobia. For example, if someone experiences a panic attack in a certain place or situation, they might develop a fear of the same and avoid going there in the future.

Specific Phobia

Both social phobia and agoraphobia are complex phobias because it might be difficult to recognize their specific triggers all the time. Also, since they're wider in scope, it might be difficult to avoid these triggers. For example, if you're agoraphobic, you might not be able to predict when you're going to encounter a trigger that makes you anxious. Similarly, once you step out of the house, you might have to interact with other people at any time. Of course, certain situations make it more likely, but it's difficult to avoid social interactions completely once you're out in public.

Specific phobias, on the other hand, are known as simple phobias because they're related to extremely specific triggers—for example, snakes or other animals, heights, water, and so on. In many cases, these specific situations or creatures aren't encountered on a regular basis, thus making it easier for people to avoid these triggers and live their lives. This is also why people who suffer from complex phobias usually have a more difficult time living a normal life.

Separation Anxiety Disorder

When we're attached to someone or something, we can feel anxious or sad when separating from them. However, when this anxiety becomes excessive or persistent, we might be suffering from separation anxiety disorder.

Although this condition is more common in children, it can also affect adults. Some of the symptoms to look out for are

- worrying excessively when thinking of separating from someone or something
- imagining extreme scenarios in which you might lose or be separated from the "attachment figure"
- feeling excessive fear related to being alone or away from the attachment figure
- unwilling to sleep away from the attachment figure
- exhibiting certain physical or emotional behaviors repeatedly when anticipating—or going through—separation from a loved one or cherished place.
- having nightmares before, during, and/or after the separation

If you've gone through certain traumatic incidents in the past—especially those involving the loss of someone close to you—you might develop separation anxiety when it comes to people you love. Similarly, if you're someone who takes a long time to feel comfortable in a new place, you might be more likely to experience separation anxiety when leaving an old one behind.

Anxiety-Related Disorders

Initially, both OCD and PTSD were classified as anxiety disorders but are now dealt with separately. Even so, anxiety is one of the main aspects of these conditions. For example, OCD in most people is characterized by the presence of persistent intrusive thoughts. These thoughts lead to fear and anxiety, which are usually alleviated through repetitive behaviors.

PTSD, on the other hand, occurs when the mind has difficulty processing some kind of trauma. This could be due to events like accidents, wars, disasters, abuse of any kind, or loss. Symptoms could include—having trouble sleeping because of nightmares or night terrors, having issues relaxing in general, and developing specific phobias related to the incident.

UNDERSTANDING SOCIAL ANXIETY

As we've discussed earlier, it's natural to feel anxious when you're dealing with a social interaction that means a lot to you. Sometimes, when we're amidst people we don't know, we might feel apprehensive about how we come across. After all, everyone wants to make a good first impression. However, social anxiety disorder—or social phobia—is more than the occasional pit in the stomach. Social phobia occurs when your regular social interactions make you feel conscious and anxious, especially because you're worried about being judged negatively by others.

Before we go any further, it's important to distinguish introversion from social anxiety. Introverts might also avoid social situations more often than others, but that doesn't mean they're socially anxious. In fact, introversion is a trait that many people are born with. Also, introversion doesn't look the same for everyone. Some people are more introverted than others. Some are ambiverts, meaning they can be extroverted in some situations and introverted in others. The main characteristic of introverts is that they generally tend to value their inner lives way more than their social lives. This is why they choose to keep their social interactions limited, and they also focus more on the quality and depth of these interactions.

Some of the characteristics of introverts are as follows:

- They might be more interested in thinking, writing, journaling, and having deep conversations with a smaller group of people instead of spending time with strangers or making small talk.

- They might even enjoy contemplating and daydreaming, as that gives them time and space to understand themselves and their feelings.
- They might want to work alone rather than in groups so that they can focus their energy properly.
- In general, most social interactions drain their energy, which means they might need some time to step back and recharge themselves in solitude.

As you can see, introverts usually have a high degree of control over their actions, and they know exactly what they want from their interactions with others. This isn't the case with socially anxious people. In fact, people who suffer from social anxiety might take extreme steps to avoid interacting with people simply because they're not sure about how they'll behave in such situations. In other words, they might experience an absolute lack of control in social situations.

Here are some characteristics of social anxiety:

- feeling extremely anxious and fearful before and during a certain event
- anticipating negative judgment from people during social interactions
- having intense fear around making mistakes or making a fool of oneself at social events
- avoiding talking to strangers
- avoiding the "spotlight" as much as possible, which means not speaking up or doing anything that might attract attention
- believing that people can see exactly how anxious they are, especially through physical symptoms such as sweating, trembling, and blushing
- engaging in negative thought patterns such as catastrophizing, overgeneralization, and fortune-telling
- overanalyzing every social interaction for days afterward in a bid to prove that they made mistakes

In chapter four, we'll also discuss how social anxiety is more than shyness.

SOCIAL ANXIETY IN WOMEN VERSUS MEN

Research shows that men and women face social anxiety differently. For one, women have a greater tendency to be socially anxious than men. The lifetime prevalence of social anxiety in women is 5.67%, as compared to 4.20% in men. Not only that, but social anxiety in women leads to lower psychosocial functioning as compared to men. This means that social anxiety hampers women's ability to form meaningful social relationships and perform their daily activities effectively (Xu et al., 2012).

Another interesting difference between women and men is that one of the greatest sources of social anxiety for women is the workplace or any situation where they have to interact with authority figures. In contrast, for men, this anxiety stems mainly from issues related to dating (Xu et al., 2012).

Since anxiety usually presents with different symptoms and comorbidities, researchers have tried to examine whether there are differences between men and women in these situations. For example, women usually suffer from more distress than men when they're socially anxious, their symptoms tend to be more severe, and they're at a greater risk of developing PTSD, GAD, and specific phobias related to social situations. Men, on the other hand, are more prone to developing conduct disorder—characterized by poor emotional behavior and disregard for others—and substance abuse disorders (Asher & Aderka, 2018).

Experts believe that these differences can occur due to various reasons, including the social conditioning that both men and women are subjected to. Certain behaviors are considered more appropriate for women rather than for men. Also, systemic issues can contribute to anxiety, as can the lack of psychological safety. Scientists are also trying to understand whether differences in brain chemistry could lead to differences in social anxiety behaviors between men and women. We'll be learning more about women and social anxiety in the next chapter.

THE COGNITIVE MODEL OF SOCIAL ANXIETY

In a bid to understand how social anxiety can affect our cognition, researchers have come up with various models over the years. One of the most popular—and oldest—models is known as the Clark and Wells model, which was developed in 1995. Most of the later models also share many of the points discussed in this model.

According to this model, people with social anxiety put too much pressure on themselves to come across as perfect. In other words, they believe that they need to be perfect in order to make meaningful social connections with others. Ironically, this obsession with seeming perfect is something that can exacerbate their anxiety and make them perform worse than usual.

Another important aspect of social anxiety is that most socially anxious people constantly look inward to assess how they're doing socially—meaning they don't pay attention to people's actual reactions and behaviors as much as their own feelings. For example, they might think, "I'm coming across as anxious and awkward," or "People think I'm behaving weirdly." These statements seem true to socially anxious people, and they don't care to check if they're true. For example, people might not be thinking that they're socially awkward, or they might not be laughing at them, but they don't know this because they're not willing to get out of their own heads.

In general, socially anxious people aren't receptive to new information, especially that comes from external sources. If ever they listen to or focus on something, it would be something related to the negative self-image they have. For example, if they think that people can notice how nervous they are—and someone casually asks if they're alright—they might conclude that their nervousness is extremely visible.

As you can see, these thinking patterns usually act as self-fulfilling prophecies, and every mistake made seems to corroborate what they actually think of themselves. Also, since they usually never try to challenge their beliefs by interacting with people, they don't have opportunities to prove themselves wrong.

An important aspect of the cognitive model relates to safety and avoidant behaviors, which we'll be discussing in detail toward the end of the chapter.

PHYSIOLOGICAL SYMPTOMS OF SOCIAL ANXIETY

Since social anxiety usually comes with feelings of distress and emotional chaos, it can affect the normal functioning of the body as well. Some of the physiological symptoms—which manifest physically and mentally—of social anxiety are

- blushing,
- trembling,
- dizziness or light-headedness,
- dry mouth,
- sweating—either excessively or in specific areas such as the palms,
- elevated heart rate,
- tightness in the chest,

- tension in the muscles or rigidity in the body, especially in the shoulders,
- having difficulty focusing on things and thinking clearly, and
- being unable to speak or stuttering while doing so.

THE ROLE OF AVOIDANCE AND SAFETY BEHAVIORS IN MAINTAINING SOCIAL ANXIETY

When people suffer from social anxiety, they tend to avoid situations that they think might exacerbate these symptoms. There are three main types of avoidance behaviors:

- **Avoidance**—People with extreme social anxiety usually try to completely avoid any situation where they might need to interact with people. Of course, anyone who's socially anxious might look for ways to avoid social interactions. This could include parties and gatherings, eating out at restaurants, dating, family reunions, and even interviews. In some cases, people also avoid taking phone calls if they can. Similarly, some people might be scared to run errands because they might meet someone they know, or they might have to engage in small talk with people who run the stores or shops.

- **Escape**—In situations where they can't completely avoid a situation, socially anxious might try to escape it. For example, they might show up at a party but leave as soon as possible. Or, they might show up at an event but spend most of their time hiding from people.
- **Safety behaviors**—In cases where they cannot either avoid a situation or escape from it, people can adopt certain behaviors that help alleviate their anxiety in the short term. The aim is to avoid attracting any attention toward oneself. For example, some people might experience selective mutism or speak so softly that people can barely hear them. Others might try to avoid eye contact so that they don't feel judged or scrutinized by the people they're interacting with. The logic behind using safety behaviors is that if they're not interacting "normally" or openly with people, they feel like they're in control of their anxiety levels.

There are many concerns about using avoidance and safety behaviors to manage social anxiety. One, these behaviors tend to make us feel more conscious of how people see us. For example, some people wear heavy makeup because they don't want people to "see" them, especially if they're prone to blushing during social interactions. The thing is, they'll become extremely conscious about using makeup every time to keep others from judging them. If someone feels like they're not doing enough to keep people from noticing their anxiety, it might actually increase their anxiety.

Two, safety and avoidance behaviors can make it very difficult to understand how people truly perceive us. For example, when we leave a party early or avoid going to one, we have no way of knowing if we would have had a good time there or met someone we genuinely enjoyed communicating with. Similarly, when we try to hide ourselves or minimize our presence in front of others, we're doing nothing to challenge our preconceived notions about how they view us. In fact, we might be unintentionally conveying to them that we're not interested in talking to *them*, which can come across as insulting and rude. For example, if we always decline invitations to events or leave events early, it might seem like we're not interested in connecting with them. In these situations, we might actually end up alienating someone, which will reinforce the negative beliefs we have about our social skills.

Three, avoidance and safety behaviors can make it difficult for us to move away from social anxiety. The thing is, it can be difficult for a socially anxious person to understand whether they're projecting their own fears onto other people's reactions or if those reactions are real. This is why "exposure" to such situations might not always be useful in the beginning, because their anxiety might make them believe that other people are perceiving them in a negative manner. Since these negative patterns of thinking don't get disrupted easily, such behaviors usually contribute toward maintaining social anxiety (Rudaz et al., 2017).

It's important to understand that—as "safe" as these behaviors might make us feel in the short term—they're only reinforcing our negative thinking patterns and anxiety. Also, we can lessen or even reverse these behaviors if we commit to it. The most important thing is to allow yourself to believe that it's possible.

In this chapter, we've understood social anxiety in detail. In the next chapter, we'll be focusing on women and their relationship with social anxiety.

2

SOCIAL ANXIETY IN WOMEN

S ocial anxiety plagues both men and women; however, it seems to affect more women than men. Also, there are certain factors that lead to greater anxiety in women. In this chapter, we'll understand why social anxiety impacts women the way it does.

FACTORS CONTRIBUTING TO ANXIETY IN WOMEN

There are numerous factors that could lead to a greater incidence of anxiety in women. Let's go through some of the major ones.

The Role of Genetics

While researchers haven't yet come up with specific genes that could be responsible for social anxiety disorder, there's a general consensus among scientists that genetics play a role in the development of social anxiety disorder. According to research, almost one-third of the reasons behind social anxiety can be traced to your genes. This is also known as the *heritability* of your social anxiety disorder. What's more, if a first-degree relative—meaning your parent, child, or full sibling—suffers from social anxiety, you're at a much higher risk of developing the disorder yourself (Cuncic, 2021).

It's vital to note here that just because your genes affect your social anxiety doesn't mean that you cannot overcome your symptoms. Don't use it as an excuse to believe that "This is just how I'm wired," and give in to your behaviors.

Environmental Factors and Social Anxiety

An interesting difference between genetic and environmental factors is this: While our genes can affect our social anxiety symptoms in the long term, our environment plays a more immediate role in shaping our behaviors. Also, while environmental factors can be short-term, some experiences are more impactful than others. This doesn't mean that environmental factors aren't important, only that they can be overcome with time. Of course, if you've had a particularly traumatic incident that has affected you deeply—for example, years of bullying at school or abuse by a parent—you might need to get some help to believe that you're more than the worst things that have happened to you.

Our genes are also responsible for our temperament, which means that if we're prone to avoidant behaviors or have low emotional stability, our environment might affect us deeply. So, our genes can also be responsible for how our environment affects us.

According to research, there are certain environmental factors that can affect social anxiety. For example, traumatic life events, difficult social experiences with peers, emotional abuse, controlling and critical parenting styles, and even other types of abuse can have a damaging effect on us (Norton & Abbott, 2017).

According to more recent research, bullying, physical abuse, and loneliness are some of the most important psychosocial factors that can lead to social anxiety disorder. At the same time, lack of peer support and lack of parental support are the greatest socio-environmental factors that contribute to this disorder (Khan & Khan, 2020).

Even Our Hormones Play a Role

When it comes to hormones, there are two main ways to look at it. For one, women tend to experience greater hormonal changes on a regular basis. For example, pregnancy is one such event where hormonal changes occur. Similarly, our menstrual cycles can lead to hormonal fluctuations every month. Since hormones can influence moods and behaviors, they can also affect our social anxiety disorder symptoms. There are three types of hormones to consider here—sex hormones, stress hormones, and thyroid hormones.

When we experience extreme stress in our lives, our bodies release two hormones in greater quantities— cortisol and adrenaline. Cortisol is the primary stress hormone, while adrenaline is the hormone that is secreted when the body's in a fight-or-flight mode. These hormones are very useful when we're dealing with a real threat in our lives. However, in case of regularly perceived threats, our bodies could be producing too many of these hormones, which could lead to an increase in anxiety symptoms. Since social anxiety can be experienced on a regular basis, it can lead to a vicious cycle where too much anxiety due to perceived threats can cause the overproduction of these hormones, which can then lead to increased anxiety. While there are many reasons why someone might experience stress, studies have shown that women are more prone to rumination—which means they focus on negative thoughts more than men. Excessive focus on such thoughts usually leads to more stress and anxiety (Johnson & Whisman, 2013).

The two main sex hormones are testosterone and estrogen. According to research, low levels of either testosterone or estrogen can increase our anxiety levels. Also, the release of cortisol—the stress hormone—and testosterone are also linked to each other. For example, too much cortisol in our bodies can lead to lower levels of testosterone, and low testosterone levels can also lead to an automatic increase in cortisol. As you can see, this leads to another cycle where stress and sex hormones together can make you feel perpetually anxious (Cuncic, 2020b).

Sex hormones are also responsible for regulating our menstruation cycles, puberty, pregnancy, and menopause—which is why we can feel more anxious during these times.

Thyroid hormones are the third kind of hormone that could be affecting our social anxiety. When our thyroid hormones are produced in higher quantities, they can lead to physiological symptoms such as shaking, increased heart rate and palpitations, and sweating.

These symptoms might, in turn, exacerbate your social anxiety behaviors.

The good news is your hormones can also be responsible for alleviating your anxiety symptoms. For example, greater levels of both testosterone and estrogen can help us feel calmer and more in control of our anxiety. Oxytocin and vasopressin are two other hormones that can help relieve anxiety. Vasopressin is associated with sexual motivation, pair bonding, maternal responses to stress, and social behavior. Oxytocin is popularly known as the "love hormone" because it's released during hugging, contact between mother and child, and interactions where we feel safe and loved. Higher levels of oxytocin in our bodies can make us feel more relaxed in social situations, thus helping reduce social anxiety.

The Connection Between Social Anxiety and Post-Traumatic Stress Disorder

Both PTSD and SAD seem to be connected to each other. On the one hand, people with PTSD have a greater chance of suffering from social anxiety. On the other hand, people with SAD can also suffer from PTSD. While most studies have different conclusions regarding the rates of people with PTSD who also suffer from social anxiety, the range is between 14–46% (McMillan et al., 2014).

Why is it more common for people with PTSD to suffer from social anxiety? When people experience traumatic situations, it can be isolating to live with the symptoms —especially if they're related to violent behavior. People with PTSD usually struggle with shame and/or guilt, both due to the traumatic incident and due to their symptoms. So, they might avoid interacting with people and being a part of social situations.

When we flip the question to: "Can people with social anxiety experience PTSD?" things get a bit trickier. This is because trauma—as defined in PTSD—usually refers to violence of any kind, death, and injury. This is why most experts aren't sure if "social trauma" could lead to the development of PTSD symptoms. However, others believe that PTSD is as much about our processing of what happens to us as it is about the event itself. This is why the same event might not have the same effect on different people. Therefore, when it comes to social trauma, you should learn to trust your gut. If it's affected you negatively, then there's a good chance that it might be responsible for your social anxiety. This has been backed by recent research, which says that social trauma—caused due to humiliating or difficult social experiences—can cause people with SAD to be more prone to experiencing PTSD. What's more, some people might even experience SAD and

PTSD as one condition rather than as separate ones (Bjornsson et al., 2020).

How Does Society Influence Social Anxiety in Women?

Apart from the socio-environmental factors that we discussed earlier, societal expectations could also be responsible for increased social anxiety in women. For example, social anxiety usually begins in adolescence, and that's when it can seem least manageable as well. This is because this is the stage at which we're beginning to form relationships that we think we're going to hold on to for life. This is also when we start seeing ourselves as "social objects" for the first time. The pressures to look a certain way, behave a certain way, and follow the rules of social interactions—whether explicit or otherwise—also become evident at this age. Of course, men go through their own share of challenges when it comes to social expectations. For women, however, there's generally a lot more scrutiny around their social success.

Not only that, but many of us begin to form romantic and platonic attachments on our own. This can lead to a whole new set of pressures to be "perfect." The popularization of social media doesn't help us. When women see the "ideals" set by society and try to conform to them, it leads to anxiety. Those who don't fit the mold or don't want to do so usually deal with more challenges than others. However, it's also vital to note that adolescence is a phase when most of us are still developing a sense of self. We're not sure of who we are or about our place in this world. This is why most of these issues can seem more challenging at this stage.

Women and Impostor Syndrome

Most people who're socially anxious believe that they're not capable enough or that they can't hold a conversation. Others believe that they're not worthy enough to fit in with a group of people. Many socially anxious people also think that it's a matter of time before they're "found out" and ridiculed. All of these characteristics are also related to impostor syndrome.

Impostor syndrome refers to the feelings we experience when we doubt our qualities and abilities and when we feel like a fraud. People who suffer from impostor syndrome have a tough time believing anyone who says that they're talented or that they deserve recognition, money, or an award. They tend to credit any success they achieve to luck while taking the blame for all mistakes and failures. Of course, almost all of us have met this monster at least once in our lives. However, it's usually more commonly experienced by women, especially because they might have to deal with more naysayers and detractors on a regular basis.

A recent KPMG study showed that 75% of women executives in the US have dealt with impostor syndrome throughout their careers. What's more, a whopping 81% believe that they need to keep reminding themselves not to fail, whereas men don't really put this much pressure on themselves (*KPMG Study Finds 75% of Executive Women Experience Imposter Syndrome,* 2020). If impostor syndrome can affect women who are seemingly excelling in their careers, no one is exempt from it. Impostor syndrome puts us in a perpetual state of "I'm not good enough," which makes it difficult for us to be our best selves socially.

Understanding the Impact of Your Temperament

Your temperament is made up of innate characteristics that stay with you in most—if not all—situations. Your temperament is mostly related to genetics, but your environment can also play a role in how it shows up throughout your life. Since your temperament is your inherent nature, it can have a huge effect on your social anxiety disorder. Your behaviors or learned patterns of thinking can, on the other hand, be changed over time. In this section, we'll discuss three aspects of your temperament and behavior that can affect your social anxiety.

Behaviorally Inhibited Temperament

Some people are born with this temperament, which means that they usually experience distress, shyness, and nervousness when faced with new and unfamiliar situations. Many people might also learn to remove or hide themselves from scenarios that make them feel uncomfortable. What's more, such traits can be seen as early as infancy, and they can have a huge impact on the development of social anxiety disorder later in life. Of course, not everyone who's behaviorally inhibited becomes socially anxious as an adult. This is also why some people who are shy aren't socially anxious.

Insecure Attachment Styles

Some children are extremely attached to their care-givers, especially when they're in the presence of strangers. These children have an anxious-ambivalent insecure attachment style, which means that they're usually unwilling to interact with strangers even when they know their caregivers—people they're attached to and trust—are present with them.

On the other hand, some children develop an anxious-avoidant insecure attachment style, which means that they exhibit indifference toward both strangers and their caregivers. This avoidant behavior is a safety behavior that makes them feel less anxious in social situations. In other words, they pretend not to care about anyone so that their fears related to social performance aren't made obvious. Doing this usually reduces their anxiety in the short term but can make them socially anxious in the long term. Children with insecure attachment styles are usually more prone to developing social anxiety disorder (Brumariu & Kerns, 2008).

Negative Beliefs and Thought Patterns

Just like some of us use avoidance behaviors to cope with social anxiety, many of us also use negative beliefs to help us deal with our anxiety. In some ways, we assume that being critical of ourselves will take away some of the sting from others' (anticipated) behavior toward us. These beliefs are usually the result of low self-esteem, certain past experiences, avoidance, and impostor syndrome.

Think about it this way. If you've gone through a humiliating experience in the past, or if you've grown up being ridiculed for something, you know how painful that experience can be. In order to protect yourself, you'll likely come up with justifications for that kind of behavior—which usually involves blaming yourself—or you'll play vivid scenes in your head regarding what *can* happen when you put yourself out there. Some of the negative beliefs that we might use to cope with social anxiety are:

- I don't fit in anywhere.
- There's something inherently wrong with me/I'm broken/I'm just not likable.
- It's obvious to others that I'm nervous, anxious, and/or awkward.
- I don't have anything to offer/I'm not going to be contributing anything worthwhile to the discussion.
- It's only a matter of time before I do something silly or embarrassing.

The thing is, when you beat yourself up like this, you might feel temporarily relieved as it means you don't have to test your social skills or even be a part of social scenarios. However, just like avoidance and safety behaviors, these thoughts can make it difficult for you to get over your social anxiety. What's more, some of these thoughts can even act as self-fulfilling prophecies —which means you can end up behaving in a manner that makes you feel like your worst thoughts about yourself are true.

Poor Self-Esteem and Self-Criticism

While this is related to negative beliefs and thought patterns, I want to discuss this separately. One of the main reasons why women have greater self-esteem issues is that they're held to higher standards in certain areas of their lives. For example, women are supposed to always come across as pleasant and agreeable and to never exhibit discomfort openly. Also, women are supposed to be "perfect" in certain roles—such as the role of a mother. This pressure to look "put-together" at all times can make women feel more like "social objects" as they increase their social interactions. This is why they might ruminate more on how they come across to others.

Usually, even mothers, aunts, and other female elders in the family tend to saddle girls with expectations regarding their behavior and image. What's worse is that over time, these criticisms or admonishments can become internalized. We might not even be able to distinguish between our own voices and those of others. When we start living with the voice inside our head that says, "You're never going to be good enough," we might start avoiding any situation that might prove the voice right. Also, perfection—by definition—cannot be achieved, so we're fighting a losing battle against ourselves that only increases our anxiety over time.

Another way in which poor self-esteem can affect women is that it tells us that we don't *deserve* to get better or get help. It tells us that we deserve whatever's happening to us and that, somehow, we're responsible for all of this. Not only does this delay treatment (if needed), but it also makes us feel comfortable in our anxiety.

Exploring Other Causes

Apart from the causes discussed above, there are certain other factors that could play a role in the development or maintenance of social anxiety. For example, researchers are still trying to understand how brain structure and chemistry in men and women could affect their tendencies to become socially anxious. This includes deficiencies in certain areas or functions—like the secretion of certain hormones—and hyperactivity in areas that are related to anxiety.

It's also important to understand that technology and social media have played a crucial role in exacerbating anxiety symptoms in women and young girls. Think about it. All the scrutiny, ridicule, and pressure to conform to arbitrary societal standards gets multiplied when you're staring at a screen. More importantly, social media provides distance and even anonymity to most people, which means that they can be cruel and condescending without having to face any real consequences for the damage they're doing. People who have a fragile sense of self or those who look for external validation more than most have a difficult time navigating the challenges that come with social media consumption.

Also, it's important to note that people with social anxiety aren't always exhibiting physical or physiological symptoms of anxiety. In fact, if they feel comfortable and safe with people around them, they might even come across as confident and communicative. This is why it's vital to note down the triggers that might make us more socially conscious. For example, we might be comfortable attending parties with people we're close to but have issues with attending them alone. Or, we might feel better if we're going to a conference where we've prepared adequately but might be thrown off-balance if we're supposed to make an impromptu speech. Maybe we're great with work-related communications but get anxious when it comes to personal interactions with strangers. Social anxiety isn't a one-size-fits-all condition, which means we need to pay attention to our relationship with it.

Now that we've understood how social anxiety can affect women, let's understand what cognitive behavioral therapy is and how it can help manage social anxiety.

3

THE COGNITIVE BEHAVIORAL APPROACH

In this chapter, we'll understand what cognitive behavioral therapy (CBT) is, how it can be useful for people suffering from social anxiety, and what techniques can be used to manage social anxiety.

WHAT IS COGNITIVE BEHAVIORAL THERAPY?

CBT is a talk therapy that helps us challenge our negative thoughts and feelings and replace them with positive ones. We've seen in the previous chapter how negative beliefs and thought processes can help to develop and maintain social anxiety. CBT helps us free ourselves from these vicious cycles. This therapy is usually short-term in nature, and the focus is on developing healthy thought patterns that can accompany us for life. Technically, the techniques we're going to discuss can be used by ourselves, but it's always a good idea to consult a professional so that you know exactly what to do. Also, even if we can identify our negative thought patterns, it can be difficult to overcome them in the beginning without any professional help. CBT can be done alone or in groups, based on the decision you and your therapist make.

This therapy is effective not only for social and other forms of anxiety but also for other conditions like phobias, panic disorders, bipolar disorder, borderline personality disorder, PTSD, OCD, psychosis, insomnia, schizophrenia, and addiction disorders. What's more, it can also help in managing the symptoms and pain associated with chronic fatigue syndrome, fibromyalgia, chronic pain, and irritable bowel syndrome (*Overview - Cognitive Behavioural Therapy [CBT]*, n.d.).

According to the American Psychological Association, CBT works on certain core principles:

- Emotional distress and mental health symptoms usually originate in the form of negative thoughts and beliefs.
- When these thoughts and beliefs become a regular part of your life, they can give rise to harmful behaviors, which further strengthen

the negative thoughts and trap you in a vicious cycle.

- Challenging these beliefs and replacing them with positive thoughts can help us combat the mental health issues we face.

There are some things to keep in mind before deciding if CBT is for you:

- This therapy focuses on current behavior and patterns and doesn't delve deep into your past issues. So, it might not help you heal from old wounds and past traumas.
- CBT is not a cure, and certainly not an instant one when it comes to social anxiety or other mental health issues. It can take a long time to get rid of the beliefs and thoughts that have sustained us so far.
- As with any other therapeutic method, the success of CBT sessions depends on your commitment. You have to work with your therapist, complete your exercises regularly, and continue them after your formal sessions are over.
- CBT is about you and how you think about the issues and scenarios that you're confronted with. Social anxiety—and many other mental

health issues—aren't only about you; there are other factors at play. CBT cannot help with resolving those issues.

- As helpful as CBT is, it can be extremely challenging in the beginning. This is because you need to become fully aware of all the negative thoughts that are holding you back, and then you need to work your way through them. This can bring up a lot of strong emotions and even make you uncomfortable in the beginning.

Since CBT is one of the most widely studied and used therapies today, you should certainly give it a try to help uncover your negative patterns.

COGNITIVE THERAPIES VERSUS OTHER PSYCHOTHERAPIES FOR SOCIAL ANXIETY

While cognitive and other behavioral therapies focus on challenging your current thought patterns and behaviors by providing strategies to overcome them, psychodynamic therapy can try to understand how your subconscious mind works and then relate it to the emotions and thoughts you experience. While psychodynamic therapy can help you deal with the same mental health issues—such as anxiety, depression, and eating disorders—it does so by focusing on your subconscious mind rather than your conscious behaviors.

Humanistic therapy focuses on issues related to self-worth and self-esteem, relationships, and past trauma. It helps us understand how our past could have shaped our worldview, which in turn affects our relationships with ourselves and others.

While more research is needed in this area, some studies have compared the efficacy of CBT with interpersonal psychotherapy (IPT) when it comes to social anxiety disorder. While CBT deals with negative thoughts and feelings, IPT is more concerned with interpersonal behaviors that could be contributing to SAD. One such study concluded that while both CBT and IPT led to significant improvements in the treatment of social anxiety disorder, CBT was more effective when it came to combating social phobia symptoms (Stangier et al., 2011).

CBT STRATEGIES FOR TREATING SOCIAL ANXIETY

Let's discuss some of the common CBT strategies that can help us overcome our social anxiety.

Psychoeducation

This is an essential part of CBT. Ideally, it should be the first step on your CBT journey. At this stage, your therapist will get to know you better—asking you questions about your issues, your goals and expectations regarding the sessions, and your participation in these sessions. They'll also explain to you how CBT can help with social anxiety and what the different methods are that they can use. Think of it as a conversation in which you can understand each other better. After all, the success of this therapy depends heavily on the relationship that you have with your therapist. Use this stage to ask any questions you might have regarding the process or to give any relevant information regarding your condition.

Attention Training

This is a technique that helps us move the focus away from us during social scenarios. Of course, this is challenging for anyone with social anxiety as they tend to focus a lot on themselves and how others might be perceiving them. Through this technique, we learn to listen and pay attention to how others are behaving during interactions. How does this help us? Remember our discussion on how extreme focus on ourselves can lead to avoidance and maintenance of social anxiety. This can also prevent us from understanding how people really look at us rather than how we *think* they do. Attention training can help challenge the negative cycles of thinking that we're used to and also help us create authentic relationships based on actual interactions with people.

The ABC Model

A huge aspect of social anxiety is rumination regarding your behavior after an event. While it's normal to think back and reflect on how you came across to others during a social interaction, overthinking and fault-finding doesn't help anyone. This technique helps us understand how our own beliefs can be responsible for less-than-optimal results during social situations. There are three parts to this technique:

- **A—antecedent.** This is the event that triggers the thoughts and behaviors that we need to understand.
- **B—beliefs.** After identifying the past event, we identify the beliefs that were related to this

event. For example, you could have believed that you were going to embarrass yourself at this event. Or, you could have decided that you wouldn't find anyone who resonated with you at the event. Some of these beliefs might be obvious, while others might be subconscious. It's important to identify these beliefs so that we can understand how they impact our behaviors during certain events.

- **C—consequence**. Now, we pay attention to our behaviors during these events and how they impact our interactions in social scenarios.

When we work through these steps, we'll understand how our own beliefs create our realities. This will help us take accountability for our behaviors before, during, and after social situations.

SMART Goal-Setting

This technique focuses on changing our behaviors in a goal-oriented manner. Usually, when it comes to social anxiety, we might want to overcome our symptoms and connect with people on a deeper level.

However, we don't know where to begin or what specific actions to take. SMART goals stand for:

- specific
- measurable
- achievable
- realistic
- time-bound

Let's try to understand this technique with an example. You want to speak up more at work but don't know how to do this. You can set goals with your therapist. Your goal could be: "I will spend an hour at lunch every week trying to talk to another colleague or a mentor. I will do this by inviting them to lunch with me." Here, the goal is to start initiating conversations with those you work with. For this, you will complete a specific task of inviting one person for lunch once a week for an hour. This goal is easily measurable and is also doable. Is it realistic? Think about how your colleagues spend time with each other during lunch. Does your office have a culture where people are usually warm and friendly? Have you ever been invited to hang out with people and have declined it before? If yes, then there's a good chance that people would love to spend time with you in a more relaxed setting. You can also set a time limit to this goal; for example, you might want to do this exercise for three months and track your progress over time. During this time, you could even write down how you feel before asking someone out for lunch, during your conversation with them, and after the conversation.

Do you feel more confident over time? Do you share some laughs or have a great conversation with someone? Do you realize you have a lot in common with someone? Chances are, your interactions will be much better than anticipated, and even the ones that don't go well wouldn't be as bad as you thought they would. In other words, you'll likely have a more objective sense of how you are as a communicator.

Cognitive Restructuring

This is an extremely useful technique that's a part of many CBT sessions. As we've discussed, the main reasons for our social anxiety are the negative thoughts and feelings that constantly plague us. Not only are these thoughts negative but they're also inaccurate. They present a distorted view of ourselves and others in social situations. Cognitive restructuring helps us challenge these thoughts and feelings and replace them with more objective ones. It's crucial to note here that we don't force ourselves to feel positive about scenarios or about ourselves. All we do is stop thinking in terms of extremes and look at things in a more neutral light.

What are some common cognitive distortions that we might need to work on?

- **All-or-nothing thinking**—This thinking pattern tells us that we're either amazing and perfect or we're absolutely worthless. This is the kind of thinking that perfectionists might experience. There's no room for mistakes, which can make us think that we're better off not trying in the first place. For example, we might think, "I wasn't able to get rapturous applause for my speech, which means I tanked my presentation."
- **Black-and-white thinking**—This is similar to all-or-nothing thinking, but here we look at people and scenarios as either good or bad. We don't allow for gray areas at all. For example, we might not get along with someone, or we might have a disagreement with someone. Instead of thinking that this is one incident, we might start doubting the person as a whole. Similarly, if a social interaction doesn't go as per our plan, we might think of it as a terrible interaction, even if it wasn't that bad.
- **Catastrophizing**—In this kind of thinking, we usually fixate on the worst-case scenario and treat it as reality. For example, we might think

that the moment we take the stage, we'll make a huge mistake, people will laugh at us, and our reputation will be ruined forever. Rationally, we know that there's a very small chance of this happening, and even then, people's memories are more fickle than we think. However, our anxiety doesn't allow us to entertain this possibility.

- **Overgeneralization**—This thinking pattern makes us believe that one incident is symptomatic of all incidents. For example, if you make a mistake, you might think, "I always mess up." Or, you might have a bad experience with someone and think, "I always attract terrible people." Overgeneralizing keeps you from taking chances on people and on yourself.

- **Personalization**—This cognitive distortion makes us believe that we're responsible for everything and everything's happening to us. For example, if we don't have a great meeting with someone, we tend to find fault with ourselves and forget that there were two people in that meeting. In some scenarios, we might not understand that the other person might be preoccupied or going through their own issues. Instead, we might blame a less-than-amazing conversation on ourselves. Or, if someone criticizes something we've done (in a respectful manner), we might assume that they have a problem with us or they don't like us.

- **Mental filtering**—This kind of thinking pattern makes us focus only on the negative aspects of a scenario, ignoring the positive parts. For example, if we're giving a speech and we make a mistake, we might focus extensively on it after the speech. In this process, we might forget that we made some great points during the speech or that people seemed to be enjoying the presentation for the most part. We might even dismiss anyone who tries to remind us of anything positive that happened during the event.

Steps to Cognitive Restructuring

Here are some steps you can take to restructure your negative thinking patterns:

- **Self-monitoring**—You can start by paying attention to how you think or behave in certain situations. It's a good idea to start a journal in which you note down your thoughts and feelings regarding different scenarios. Sometimes, we don't even know how we think and how those thoughts affect us. When you do this exercise continuously for some time, you'll begin to notice certain patterns emerging. For example, you might notice that you have a tendency to overgeneralize situations. Or, you might realize that you focus exclusively on the negative aspects of a situation.

- **Socratic questioning**—This is a method by which you begin to question the assumptions underlying your negative thoughts. In this method, we keep questioning ourselves or our therapist questions us until thoughts are either proven to be true or their distortions are made clear to us. Some of the questions we can ask ourselves at this stage are: "Do you have any evidence backing this thought?" "Are you stating facts or allowing your emotions to lead the way?" "Have you tried to check in with people you trust regarding the assumptions you've made?" "Is there a way to corroborate or refute this belief?" "What's the worst that will happen if you let go of this belief?" "Is there another way of looking at things?"
- **Looking for other perspectives**—People with anxiety are usually trapped in an echo chamber of their own making. Usually, the only voice they hear is their own. Even if they allow other voices inside, these voices only seem to

corroborate what they already feel about themselves. So, it's important to listen to people and start "gathering evidence" against these voices. Talk to people you trust and ask them what they think about your social skills. What do they like most about you? What do they think you bring to a conversation? Do they think your "flaws" are deal breakers? You can also discuss an event that you think turned out badly for you and ask them to give their opinion on it. When you listen to kind and honest voices, you'll likely begin to notice the inaccuracies in your own thinking patterns.

- **Emotional reframing**—Once we've identified our negative thoughts and feelings, we need to look for alternative ways of thinking, feeling, and talking about our experiences. We can identify the cognitive distortion that is affecting us and then reframe it to a more neutral thinking pattern. For example, if we're used to all-or-nothing thinking, we might say something like, "Well, this event was a disaster." After reframing, we can say, "Well, it didn't go as I would have liked it to go, but there were some good things about it."

Exposure Therapy

Since avoidance behaviors can usually help in maintaining social anxiety, exposure therapy can help us overcome our social phobia and anxiety by "exposing" us to situations that we're wary of. Apart from social anxiety disorder, exposure therapy can also help us deal with specific phobias, OCD, PTSD, GAD, and panic disorder. The main aim of exposure therapy is to make us feel less scared of social situations by making us face them for a prolonged period of time. While you can do this yourself, it's advisable to consult a professional and work with them, at least in the beginning. This is because certain situations might end up triggering us more than we expected them to, and it might be difficult for us to contain our emotional, physiological, and physical responses during that time.

Types of Exposure Therapy

Depending on how we're exposed to our fears, there are three main types of exposure therapy:

- **Imaginal exposure**—In this method, the socially anxious person is asked to rely on their imagination and think about situations that cause them anxiety. They're encouraged to describe these situations in great detail so that they might feel like they're currently facing the situation.

- **In vivo exposure**—This method exposes the socially anxious person to real-life situations that elicit anxiety. For example, they might be asked to go to a party once a week. Or, they might be asked to give a presentation at work. If they're worried about making small talk with strangers, they might be asked to approach one stranger and initiate small talk with them.
- **Interoceptive exposure**—In this technique, the focus is on making the individual understand that the physical and physiological symptoms associated with social anxiety are harmless. Sometimes, when socially anxious people start sweating or have a panic attack, they might get scared, thinking that something's wrong with them or that they're going to be hurt. By introducing these sensations in a controlled environment, the therapist normalizes them for the individual.
- **Virtual exposure**—In some situations, it's better for the socially anxious person to be exposed to the scenario in a virtual environment. Here, the person feels like they're a part of the situation while also knowing that no real "harm" can come to them. It's more

controlled than in vivo exposure and might be a good idea in the beginning.

Depending on the pace that you and your therapist agree on, you can also be exposed to your sources of anxiety in various ways:

- If you experience **flooding**, you'll be exposed to your worst fears first and then to lesser fears.
- **Graded exposure** works in the opposite way, meaning that you'll be exposed to situations that invoke the least amount of fear and then gradually exposed to those that are scarier than the previous ones.
- If you undergo **systematic desensitization**, you'll be exposed to your fears and then given relaxation exercises to deal with the ensuing anxiety.

Benefits of Exposure Therapy

Once people get used to the social scenarios that they fear and avoid, they'll find themselves getting less anxious over time. They'll also notice that their emotional and physical responses are getting weaker over time. Repeated exposure to difficult scenarios also means that people begin to notice the cracks in their own reasoning. For example, someone who thinks that people don't enjoy spending time with them might notice after many meetings that they're mistaken. Similarly, someone who once thought that public speaking was scary will probably realize that it's not as bad as they thought it to be.

This way, they might start reframing their own negative beliefs and thought patterns over time. Also, people with social anxiety might feel extremely helpless in the face of their symptoms. The moment they experience these symptoms, they might believe that avoidance, escape, or safety behaviors are their only options. Therefore, in the beginning, they might have to deal with their helplessness. However, with time, they might gain confidence in their abilities to deal with difficult situations as well as their own emotional responses to them.

According to research, exposure therapy is useful in reducing social anxiety and in reducing cognitive, behavioral, and affective symptoms related to anxiety (Scheurich et al., 2019).

Mindfulness-Based Techniques

Why is mindfulness useful for people with social anxiety? Since anxiety stems from the fact that we spend a lot of time ruminating about difficult scenarios, we need to be present in the moment and focus on what we can control. The truth is a lot of things will always be out of our control. However, the more we make peace with this, the better we get at dealing with our anxiety. Here's where mindfulness comes in. It helps us pay attention to our triggers, emotions, and thoughts without judging ourselves for feeling a certain way. This is important because the more we judge ourselves, the more difficult it gets to escape this vicious cycle.

According to a study, mindfulness meditation is useful for reducing anxiety, depression, and rumination in socially anxious people. At the same time, it can help in increasing our self-esteem as well (Goldin et al., 2009).

When you're getting started with mindfulness-based practices, there are some things to keep in mind:

- Mindfulness is less about a particular practice and more about **the understanding you bring to a situation**. When you do anything mindfully, you focus your attention on it and try to enjoy the process without worrying too much about the past or the future. Think about the different activities you can do with mindfulness.
- No matter what you think, it's always a good idea to **be aware of your breath**. Not only does this calm you down, but it also gives you an

anchor that can keep you in place when your mind starts wandering. For example, if you're thinking about the last time you tried to have a conversation with someone and it didn't go too well, you might feel a surge of unpleasant emotions arising within you. At this time, it's a good idea to simply focus on your breath and let those emotions move through you. This way, you won't be shutting down in the face of emotions, nor will you let these emotions overwhelm and unmoor you.

- You can also use a **guided meditation or a script** to help you in the beginning. This way, you won't be distracted too often, and you'll also feel like someone's guiding you through the process. If you can, you can also look for meditation classes near you so that you get more comfortable working through your emotions in public.

- **Experiment** with different timelines, locations, and activities. You will take some time to understand what works for you, and that's perfectly alright.

Apart from mindfulness meditation, here are a few relaxation techniques that can help you cope with social anxiety.

Belly Breathing

Any kind of deep breathing practice can be extremely useful in dealing with social anxiety. One of these exercises is called belly—or diaphragmatic—breathing. Here, your stomach rises and falls during breathing, expanding your diaphragm and allowing more air to enter your body. This is a deeper form of breathing than the usual practice of breathing through the chest. Since anxiety attacks usually cause our breathing to become shallower, belly breathing can help in making us feel less anxious.

Body Scan

A body scan is a simple technique that helps you focus on your body and understand how it reacts to anxiety. This practice can also help you ground yourself when you're feeling particularly anxious. All you need to do is to start breathing deeply and focus your attention on various parts of your body. As you inhale, you understand how your body is dealing with stress and anxiety —whether it has become painful or more tense in any way. If yes, then you release that tension with each exhale.

Progressive Muscle Relaxation

During progressive muscle relaxation, you will induce relaxation throughout your body. For this, you need to focus on specific muscle groups and then alternately contract and relax these muscles. When you do this, your body enters a relaxed state and you feel less anxious.

Visualization or Guided Imagery

Sometimes, thinking about situations where we've been humiliated or where we anticipate embarrassment can exacerbate our anxiety symptoms. During these times, it can be helpful to imagine ourselves in a place or situation where we feel relaxed. Think about something that makes you feel at ease with yourself. Do you imagine yourself at the beach? Do you visualize yourself breathing in the fresh morning air? Are you most peaceful when surrounded by your favorite people in the world? Just as you tend to obsess over the details of anxiety-inducing social situations, so too you should spend time going into the details of this imaginary world that makes you feel less anxious. Of course, you should be careful about doing this exercise only when you're in a safe space.

SOCIAL SKILLS TRAINING

Social skills training is also a behavioral therapy that helps socially anxious people to work on their social skills with the help of a therapist. These sessions can be done individually as well as in groups, but most therapists prefer a mixture of both. In the initial sessions, we discuss the skills that we would really like to focus on and improve. After that, the therapist uses a few techniques to help us become more confident with our social skills:

- **Modeling of appropriate behaviors**—Through in-person or video sessions, therapists help individuals to understand how to behave appropriately in different situations. For example, they could show them how to introduce themselves to strangers, how to make small talk with them, how to read the room and avoid making inoffensive statements, and how to use humor in an appropriate manner.
- **Scripts**—One of the ways to teach social skills to individuals is by making them read scripts that can give them an idea of the proper way to behave in social situations.
- **Role plays**—Through this technique, the therapist and the individual can go through

certain scenarios and act out how they would behave in these situations.

- **Feedback and reinforcement**—Throughout the sessions, it's important for the socially anxious person to get feedback on what they can improve. Also, if they've successfully learned something or made progress in learning a certain skill, they need to be recognized for that.

COGNITIVE BEHAVIORAL THERAPY EXERCISES FOR YOU

Now that we've learned what CBT is and how it can be useful in combating social anxiety, let's go through two exercises that you can do on your own.

Journaling About Your Anxiety

One of the most helpful exercises to deal with anxiety is to start journaling about your experiences. While it's true that social anxiety—or at least parts of it—looks or feels similar for many people, there are experiences and sensations that are unique only to you.

When you start making a note about your experiences, try to answer a few of these questions:

- What are the specific events that trigger your anxiety?
- What are the feelings and sensations you experience before the event?
- What do you do to cope with these feelings?
- Do you talk to someone when you feel this way or do you try to deal with it alone?
- What are the reasons you feel this way about certain events?
- What are your worst fears regarding these situations?
- Have you ever tried to challenge these fears?
- Is there anything that makes you feel less anxious during the event?
- How many of these things are dependent on others and how many have to do with you?
- What are the underlying thoughts behind your anxieties?
- Have you tried replacing these thoughts or behaviors with alternative ones?

Remember not to judge yourself for any of the answers. It's important to give yourself the grace to feel these things and then think about how to overcome them.

Also, don't rush to solutions in the beginning. It's vital to stay in these difficult emotions and understand yourself before you try to "fix" yourself.

A Different Perspective

How many times have you seen your worst fears come alive in your head—like a horror movie you didn't buy the tickets to? How about we change the script? Use your powerful imagination to create a movie where you are successful and everything works out for you. Think about how you would feel if you gave an amazing speech at work and people came up to you to say how much you inspired them. Imagine yourself having a stimulating conversation with someone and getting to know them at a deeper level. How would you feel during and after that conversation? Imagine yourself being the center of attention at a gathering and enjoying this chance to connect with others. Admittedly, some of these scenarios will be more challenging to imagine than others. However, you should give yourself time to relax and think about these situations in detail. There's a lot of power in visualization because our brains don't always understand the difference between real life and visualization. So, if you do this exercise regularly, you'll likely start believing that this could be your reality.

In the next chapter, we'll discuss strategies other than CBT that can help us cope with social anxiety.

4

DEALING WITH YOUR SOCIAL ANXIETY

Now that we've understood how CBT can be helpful in managing social anxiety, let's look at some other techniques that we can employ to do so.

ARE YOU JUST SHY?

Before we move on to different coping techniques, let's understand the difference between shyness and social anxiety. Many people confuse social anxiety for shyness, which puts them at a disadvantage and prevents them from getting the help they need. It's usually easy to notice someone who is shy. These people will usually feel nervous in social situations and wouldn't want people to notice them or focus their attention on them. Many shy people would be very happy being invisible. In many cases, shyness stems from low self-esteem. Shy people are usually worried about how people see them and whether they're making a good impression or not.

I know that this sounds very similar to social anxiety. However, the difference between the two conditions lies in the intensity of the fear or anxiety that a person experiences in social situations. Also, shy people aren't as avoidant as socially anxious people, and their shyness doesn't usually disrupt their lives to the extent that social anxiety does (Heiser et al., 2009).

It's important to understand that shyness is a personality trait while social anxiety is a mental health condition. Consequently, shyness doesn't need to be treated, while social anxiety disorder can get worse without treatment. Also, both social anxiety and shyness can be situational. For example, someone who feels shy at the beginning of an event can get more comfortable by the end of it. Or, they can feel shy around strangers but open up after some time and have a great time talking to them.

Social anxiety is also brought about by different situations, but the feelings and negative thoughts can plague us before, during, and after the situation. Also, it's usually much easier for people to evolve from shyness. For example, many children are extremely shy but grow up to be confident adults without any major interventions.

It's crucial to pay attention to your symptoms if you're shy. For example, ask yourself if your shyness affects you for days before an event, or does it make you want to stop going out completely? Do you spend a lot of time thinking about how people perceive you, or do you generally deal with a lot of negative thoughts? If yes, it might be a good idea to get yourself tested. If your doctor rules out social anxiety, then you might simply need to work on getting more comfortable in your skin and confident in your communication skills.

MEASURING SOCIAL FUNCTIONING

There are many scales that can be used to measure your social functioning. One of the most common and effective ones is the Social Skills Inventory (SSI), developed by Ronald Riggio in 1986. This is a self-assessment that can help measure social competence through six basic social skills. This test is used to help determine emotional intelligence as well as social communication skills. Individuals are judged on both nonverbal and verbal communication skills. For both these aspects, individuals are judged on control, sensitivity, and expressivity. While sensitivity focuses on how receptive they are to what other people are saying, expressivity is about how well you can talk to others. Control refers to the management of both nonverbal and verbal skills during communication. This is a useful test to take to understand what our strengths and weaknesses are with regard to social skills.

An interesting study was done to determine the effect of social anxiety on the social skills of individuals. There were some interesting observations from the study. While socially anxious individuals might not lack social skills compared to those without anxiety, they have a tendency to rate their skills lower. Also, they might not be able to perform well in front of others because of their anxiety, which can lead to rejection and loneliness (Segrin & Kinney, 1995). So, we need to not only improve our social skills but also gain more confidence in the skills we possess.

IDENTIFYING AND CHALLENGING YOUR SOCIAL STRESSORS

Since most socially anxious people experience stress when it comes to social situations, it's important to first identify the source of stress and then come up with coping strategies for the same. This can be tough in the beginning because we don't always want to confront our stressors. However, once you know why you're feeling stressed, you'll be better equipped to deal with it and become less anxious over time.

How do you identify the source of your stress? This requires you to distance yourself from your emotions and look at situations more objectively. Journaling can help you calm down and note down the reasons behind your stress. Also, try to go deeper and don't settle for the first thing that comes to your mind. For example, you have an event coming up in the next week. Are you stressed because you don't know many people there? Are you stressed because you might have to say something at the event? Why are you stressed about speaking to a group of people? Are you not sure of the subject matter? Do you have bad memories from the last time you spoke in public? Do you have people around you who are less than encouraging when it comes to your speaking abilities?

Once you've identified what exactly it is that's stressing you out, you can try to either avoid the source of stress completely or you can tackle it head-on. For example, if possible, try to limit the number of people around you who aren't kind or encouraging. If you're stressed because you don't feel prepared enough, you can read more on the subject matter and practice more too. If you have unpleasant memories regarding the last time, try to visualize how it would feel when you give a good speech this time.

When we're stressed, we usually keep to ourselves and don't let others help us. This only serves to increase our stress levels. Instead, we should actively try to surround ourselves with people who make us feel good about ourselves. Also, if we need help with something, it's better to confide in someone we trust. Once we let someone help us, we'll automatically feel less burdened about our performance in the future.

Last but not least, we need to lower our expectations when it comes to our social performance. If we expect an amazing performance each time we take part in social interactions, we're always going to be stressed about missing the mark. Instead, we should think more about enjoying our interactions or about forming connections with others. Also, while you need to be responsible for your part of the interaction, you should also remember that any conversation requires two or more people. So, let other people also contribute toward making the interaction a success. You don't need to carry the entire conversation yourself.

NAVIGATING PANIC ATTACKS WITHOUT FEAR

Even though panic attacks can be scary, they're not harmful, and they don't imply that something is wrong with you. They're simply a symptom of extreme anxiety in the moment. When people start experiencing panic attacks, they might not know what's happening to them. If they experience this attack in a public place, they might even be embarrassed and feel like everyone's judging them for being weak. When we think this way, we become anxious about being anxious, which isn't helpful at all. So, here are some things you can do to cope with panic attacks:

- **Pay attention to your diet** and see if it has any effect on the intensity of your panic attack. This means that you should eat well and regularly so that your blood sugar levels remain stable. It also means avoiding foods that make you feel lethargic or fatigued. Limit your consumption of caffeine, tobacco, and alcohol, as they can exacerbate your panic attack symptoms.
- **Regular exercise** is also a good idea as it makes us feel calmer in general and can help reduce stress and anxiety in our daily lives.
- The first thing to do before, during, and after an attack is to **remind yourself that it's okay**

to feel this way. Don't blame yourself or feel guilty for whatever's happening to you.

- **Don't pretend that it's not happening**. Give yourself permission to feel your emotions, even as they become difficult and overwhelming. Allow that wave to pass through you and know that these feelings—however unsettling—will subside.

- During a panic attack, you need to **find ways to ground yourself**. One of the easiest ways of doing so is by focusing on your breathing. Chances are, your breathing will become really shallow during this time, so the first thing to do is to consciously start breathing more deeply. If you can, close your eyes and inhale deeply through your nose, followed by a deep exhale through your mouth. You can also count your breaths to feel more grounded.

- Some people like to **keep an object that grounds them** during this time. Do you have a favorite soft toy that makes you feel calm? You can keep it with you and use it to feel better during a panic attack.

- You can also use *mantras* **or affirmations** to ground yourself when you feel unsettled during a panic attack. When you repeat the same (positive) thing over and over—even something as simple as "It's okay," your mind starts believing you after a while and gives a signal to your body to calm down.

- Try the **5-4-3-2-1 method for grounding**. In this method, we engage all our senses to feel more connected to the world around us. This helps us get out of our head and become more comfortable in our body. The first step is to look at five different things around you and pay attention to them for some time. Then, we listen to four different sounds in our environment. After that, we touch three objects —keeping our safety in mind—and think about how they make us feel. Are they soft to the touch? Are they cool or warm? Do they have an interesting texture? Then, we move on to smelling any two things around us. Pay attention to the differences between the two smells. In the end, we try to taste any one thing available to us. Some people like to keep candies for this purpose. By the end of this exercise, you'll likely feel more in control of your emotions and symptoms.
- If you can, **choose a spot where you feel calm**. For example, if you're at home, go to a room or a corner of the house where you feel at ease. If it's safe, you can even go outside and spend

some time walking on grass barefoot. If it's not possible to physically go somewhere calming, you can try to close your eyes for a bit and visualize yourself in a calm setting. Again, do this only when you have trusted people near you or when you're in a safe, enclosed space.

WHEN EMOTIONAL REGULATION MATTERS

One of the challenges of people dealing with social (or any) anxiety is that they might have sudden and extreme reactions to their triggers. This causes them to worry about taking part in social interactions. For example, think of how children sometimes throw tantrums or become extremely fussy and unmanageable when anxious or stressed. As we grow up, we learn to regulate our emotions so that they don't become disruptive. However, extreme anxiety can sometimes short-circuit the route between our emotions and consequent reactions. This can lead to avoidance and safety behaviors that might seem to help in the short term but aren't helpful over time.

The good news is emotional regulation can be learned. Here are a few things you can do to improve your emotional regulation skills:

- **Cultivate self-awareness**—How do you become more self-aware? You confront all the parts of yourself, especially those that you don't like. Two ways of doing this are by maintaining a regular journaling practice and practicing mindfulness in your daily life. While journaling can provide insights into your own thoughts and emotions, mindfulness-based practices can help you observe yourself without judgment. This isn't as easy as it sounds, as you might come across some truly unsettling and difficult aspects of yourself. The trick lies in not abandoning yourself during these moments.
- **Practice cognitive restructuring**—When we challenge our negative thoughts and replace them with more neutral ones, we allow ourselves to pause before giving in to our worst instincts. For example, if you feel like the people around you don't like you, you might feel like running away or behaving irrationally in front of them. Instead, if you ask yourself to pause and reevaluate the situation, you might find out that people aren't hostile to you.

Maybe they're busy, or they're equally nervous. Some of them might actually be interested in learning more about you. In the beginning, it can be difficult to get into a mode of questioning your thoughts. With time, however, it'll come more easily to you.

- **Work on becoming more adaptable—** When we're plagued with doubt and anxiety, we might choose to keep ourselves comfortable at all times. Unfortunately, this means that we never challenge ourselves, nor do we open ourselves up to new experiences. This, in turn, makes every new situation that much more formidable to us. There are ways to become more flexible and adaptable when it comes to new situations so that they don't elicit extreme responses from us. For example, you can try to go to one event around you in a week. If you feel scared about going alone, take someone with you who can make you feel relaxed. If there's someone in your surroundings from a different cultural or linguistic background, try to strike up a conversation with them. You can invite them to your home for lunch or dinner, or you can take them out to your favorite restaurant. Try listening to them and get to know their experiences. They'll likely have a lot of stories about trying to fit in and deal with culture shocks. They might also talk about how enriching it is to get to know more people and become intimate with a culture that's not yours. These conversations will not only make you feel less alone, but they'll also give you much-needed perspective on pushing your limits.

- **Practice self-compassion**—Sometimes (or most times), we're unnecessarily harsh on ourselves. This can inhibit our emotional regulation over time. The more we love ourselves, the easier it'll be to deal with any difficult emotions that arise in certain situations. For this, you should regularly practice mindfulness meditation. There's a specific kind of meditation—known as metta or loving-kindness meditation—that can help you develop compassion for yourself and for others around you. This is a simple meditation in which you focus your attention on yourself or the person you want to thank. Then, as you inhale deeply, thank this person sincerely. Thank yourself for existing and showing up during the difficult times. Be grateful for whatever you can do and all the ways in which you protect yourself. Thank yourself for trying even when it's hard. Tell yourself that you deserve all the good things, even those that you're currently running away from. Whenever possible, practice gratitude for everything in your life. This way, you'll combat any feelings of low self-esteem and start counting your blessings. When you're feeling grateful, it's harder to experience blame and guilt for anything that goes or might go wrong.

- **Actively look for emotional support**—While having an extreme emotional reaction can be difficult, it's even more difficult if you have to face constant blame for it. You need to surround yourself with people who give you the strength to face your emotions without any judgment. These can be your friends, family members, or even people from your community who understand your challenges. If you don't find someone in your life who can support you through this process, look for professional help if you can afford it.

MANAGING SOCIAL SITUATIONS

Once you start exposing yourself to different social situations, you might feel overwhelmed about handling these situations with composure and elegance. While no two situations are the same, there are some things that you can keep in mind:

- **Don't rush to the event**—I know that some of us feel extremely anxious when we're late for an event. However, there's a fine line between being on time and being anxiously early. Also, many of us start fussing and worrying about doing things right long before the actual event. As counterintuitive as it might seem, try to slow yourself down. Sit down, relax, and do something that you enjoy. Eat something light but comforting if it helps. When you decide to leave for the journey, take your time and don't rush on the way. If you can, choose a route that's scenic or interesting. When you act as if the event is important but not urgent, you'll likely feel less anxious by the time you reach there.

- **There are no strangers here**—If you're going to an event where you don't really know anyone, trick your brain into thinking that that's not the case. Tell yourself that you're going to meet friends. If you don't feel this way, try to smile more often. You'll be surprised at how easily most people get disarmed when they see someone flash them a genuine smile. When people start warming up to you, it'll be easier to pretend that they're already your friends.

- **When in doubt, ask questions**—Sometimes, we put too much pressure on ourselves to say the right words. If we're unfamiliar with the topic being discussed, or we simply feel too unprepared to talk, we might keep ourselves from offering anything to the discussion. Instead of doing this, why not ask people open-ended questions? Not only does this convey interest in what the other person is saying, but it takes away the focus from us by making us the listener. Everyone likes an interested audience. Also, when you ask questions, you allow the conversation to become more exploratory in nature. In other words, the conversation becomes less predictable but not in an anxiety-inducing way.

TECHNOLOGY AND SOCIAL CONNECTION

When it comes to technology and social connection, things get a bit tricky. On the one hand, technology is responsible for making the world smaller and for bringing us closer to each other. Nowhere did we feel the power of technology than during the pandemic. When people were forced to work from home and shelter in place—not to mention having to deal with the uncertainty of the disease—it was technology that made sure we didn't feel completely alone. Even as we missed the energy of meeting people in person, we had the comfort of seeing them virtually and sharing our lives with each other during difficult times.

On the other hand, we can sometimes use technology in such a way that it leaves us feeling more isolated than usual. For example, if we spend most of our time on social media and try to compare ourselves with others, it can put a serious dent in our self-esteem. Similarly, if we use virtual connections to avoid making real-life connections with people, we might end up feeling lonely in our real lives.

A few studies have been done to examine how technology can affect social anxiety. In one study, researchers concluded that excessive smartphone use can lead to a greater risk of social anxiety in young adults (Darcin et al., 2016). Another study concluded that addiction to technology is closely related to isolation, low self-esteem, and social anxiety (Vaghefi et al., 2017).

When it comes to technology, therefore, it's important to understand why you're using it. You should also pay attention to the intention behind it, the frequency of use, and the effect it has on you. It's not a bad idea to use technology to make yourself feel comfortable talking to people. For example, you might find it easier to connect with people through a screen than in person. Or, you might be able to join online communities that make you feel safe and seen. You might feel less scrutinized when you share your experiences and have conversations with people online. However, if you begin to use social media as a measure of your worth, or if you want to hide behind the anonymity that the internet can sometimes provide you, then you're doing yourself a disservice. Remember that technology can be a great enabler and it can also be a crutch. Only you can decide what its role in your life is going to be.

Now, let's go through some exercises related to social anxiety and emotional regulation.

EXERCISES TO DEAL WITH SOCIAL ANXIETY

Here are two exercises you can do to help deal with your social anxiety.

Alternate Reality Exercise

One of the most powerful ways to overcome your social anxiety is to envision what life would look like without it. Here's a simple exercise that you can do whenever you're contemplating whether you should be a part of a social event or not.

Step 1: Think of the event that you're trying to avoid or an activity that you usually avoid doing.

Step 2: Think of the good things that you miss out on when you do so. For example, if you don't make an effort to talk to people, do you think you miss out on some amazing conversations? You can even draw upon the experiences of your friends or family members for this part. What do you think they're experiencing that you would also like to?

Step 3: This is the stage where you let your imagination run wild and think about a reality where you're not afraid of doing something or being a part of a social scenario. What would your life look like then? Would it be filled with exhilarating conversations with interesting people? Would it mean that you're open to a world of new opportunities? Would it lead to a lifelong friendship or a beautiful partnership? Don't hold back when you think about the life you want and how overcoming your social anxiety might help make this life a reality.

Note down these steps regularly and make it a point to go through them every now and then. Maybe at some point, the fear of missing out on the life of your dreams could overpower the fear of social interactions.

Experiments With Social Behavior

This is another exercise where you compare what you *think* will happen in a social scenario to what actually happens.

Step 1: Write down an action or scenario that causes anxiety within you.

Step 2: Make a note of everything you think will happen if you take part in that social activity. For example, what do you think will happen if you approach a stranger and strike up a conversation with them? Do you think they will rebuff you? Do you think they will mock you? Be as specific as you can be.

Step 3: Decide when you want to do that activity. In the beginning, you can choose an activity that doesn't cause you a lot of anxiety. This is like graded exposure therapy. For example, in the beginning, you can simply say "Hi" to or smile at a stranger.

Step 4: Write down what actually happened when you took part in that activity. Then, compare Step 4 to Step 2.

This will give you an idea about the inaccuracies in your thinking processes and encourage you to take more chances with yourself.

EXERCISES FOR EMOTIONAL REGULATION

Here are two exercises that you can do to work on your emotional regulation (Ackerman, 2023):

Labeling Your Emotions

One of the biggest challenges in learning emotional regulation is that we often categorize our emotions as either positive or negative. Also, we sometimes don't realize what exactly it is that we're feeling. Labeling your emotions can be a powerful act that also makes you realize that it's okay to feel each emotion. Not only that, but this act will give you pause and make you think before reacting to the emotion.

Whenever you feel an intense emotion, write it down without attaching a value—positive or negative—to it. Be as precise as possible. After you've gotten comfortable with this, you can start thinking of your emotions in terms of how they impact your life or what the reactions are that these emotions elicit from you. For example, what do you normally do when you're happy? What do you do when you're sad or angry? Once you've noted down your common reactions to emotions, you'll know that it's best to pause when an emotion makes you react in a way that isn't helpful.

Emotion, Action, and Opposite Action

Step 1: Write down the different emotions you experience in difficult situations.

Step 2: Write down the actions you perform or the reactions you give when faced with each emotion. You can even give specific examples to make the point clearer to you.

Step 3: Think of a different action that you can perform during this time. For example, if you usually run away from a place that is making you anxious, could you instead sit down in one place? Or, if you tend to say something rude to someone when you feel anxious, could you simply take a few deep breaths before you respond to them? Again, be as specific as possible so that you're not scrambling in the moment.

In the next chapter, we'll learn how to tackle our fears head-on.

5

LETTING GO OF YOUR FEAR

While fear is an emotion that all of us experience from time to time, it can also become the reason why we're not living life to the fullest. Many times, fear is the only thing standing between you and your dreams. It might not be possible to completely eradicate fear from our lives, but it's certainly possible to stop living in fear all the time. In this chapter, we'll try to understand how fear can negatively impact our lives and how we can prevent it from controlling our lives.

FEAR: SOMETIMES, YOU'RE HOLDING YOU BACK

Fear is often seen as a negative emotion, and with good reason. When we feel afraid, our lives seem to constrict around us. We cannot think or do anything without being plagued by fear. Like a dark cloud, it hangs over everything we do. Also, fear makes us seem weak. No one wants to admit that they're afraid, even though everyone knows that fear is a common emotion.

It seems like fear isn't useful in any way, but that's not true. Historically, fear was responsible for keeping us safe. When our ancestors were dealing with the ravages of nature or trying to protect themselves from wild animals, they needed to rely on their instincts at all times. When they felt fear, their bodies released hormones that put them in fight-or-flight mode. In other words, fear helped them prepare their bodies to deal with the numerous dangers that they faced each day.

Now, we can experience fear even if the danger is imaginary in nature. For example, if we think that all future social interactions will be terrible, we might be scared of venturing out. Even if these dangers aren't real yet, as long as they're real in our minds, we're going to experience fear.

Some common triggers for fear are

- certain objects, animals, or situations related to our phobias,
- imaginary or anticipated events,
- real dangers around you, and
- uncertainty about the future.

The symptoms of fear are similar to those of anxiety, such as chills, dry mouth, nausea, upset stomach, increased heart rate, chest pain, sweating, and trembling.

We don't experience the same level of fear in all situations. There are many reasons why we feel more fearful in some scenarios than others. For example, if the anticipated harm caused by the trigger is immediate, we'll be more fearful. Also, if we know how to cope with our fears, we'll feel more in control than if we don't. You don't need to feel ashamed about what causes you fear, but it's important to be honest with yourself about why something scares you.

PUSHING PAST YOUR FEAR

Here are some steps you can take to conquer your fears:

- **Be kind to yourself**—As with any other "negative" emotion, it can be tempting to blame yourself for how you feel during this time. You might even feel like you're letting yourself down by being scared. Instead of doing this, try to understand what your fear is telling you. Why are you scared of this particular thing or event? Since when has this particular fear plagued you? Has your fear ever been helpful to you? If yes, do you think it's still helpful? Answer these questions with compassion toward yourself.

- **Don't hide behind your fears**—There's a fine line between being kind to yourself and being overly self-indulgent. Pay attention to how your fears are getting in the way of living the life you want. Have you started making excuses to avoid facing your fears? Are there other people in your life who are enabling you instead of pushing you to overcome your fears? Try to be honest with yourself about what you're scared of and why.

- **Pay attention to your symptoms**—Fear can look different for different people. Some people might become quiet and submissive when they're scared. Others might become aggressive to hide their fear. Sometimes, it might take a while to realize that you're acting out due to fear. So, pay attention to how you react when you feel scared.

- **You don't always have to conquer fear**—Don't get me wrong; I'm not implying that it's good to live in fear. However, you need to understand that fear is a part of life. The important thing is to not let fear govern your life. If you find fear forcing you to inaction, that's when you need to worry. Learn to do things even when you're afraid of them. For example, if you're meeting someone new, you don't need to say, "I'm not scared of meeting a stranger." Instead, you can say, "I'm quite nervous and scared about this meeting but it's also a great opportunity to expand my network. So, I need to do this."

- **Look for alternative behaviors to handle your fears**—Just like with negative thoughts or anxiety, you need to look for healthy behaviors that you can practice when feeling scared. Would you like to focus on your breath? Do you have someone you can call when you're scared?

Is there a mantra you can recite at this time? Can you remind yourself to behave in a certain manner when something scares you? For example, if you're scared that people don't like you, could you flash them a smile?

- **Start small**—It takes a long time to overcome our fears, so you don't need to do everything overnight. When you start this journey, think only about the next step you need to take. Don't think about anything else at this time.

- **Celebrate every milestone**—When your life has been restricted by fear, you might forget to celebrate the small wins. For example, if your aim is to lead a discussion at work one day, don't wait to achieve that before you acknowledge your efforts. If you've started speaking up more at meetings, that's a win. If you've had a discussion with your manager about contributing more at work, that's a win too. Every time you move a little bit out of your comfort zone, give yourself a pat on your back.

COPING WITH PHYSICAL SYMPTOMS OF ANXIETY

We've previously gone through the physical symptoms of anxiety. These include sweating, trembling, increased heart rate, shallow breathing, and so on. In many cases, CBT, medication, or a combination of both can help you deal with these extreme symptoms. If you think you can manage them on your own, there are certain things that can help you. The first thing to do is to get adequate sleep during the night. You also need to be well-rested during the day and stay away from stimulants. When your body feels relaxed, it doesn't react as violently to stress or anxiety.

If you're prone to exhibiting physical symptoms of anxiety, it's a good idea to conduct a regular body scan on yourself. You can set a timer to do so, especially on days when you anticipate more stress than usual. When you find your body getting tense, there's a good chance that you're becoming anxious. When this happens, allow yourself to breathe and practice some relaxation exercises, such as progressive muscle relaxation. Most importantly, remind yourself that it's perfectly okay to feel this way and these symptoms will subside in due time.

PRACTICING EXPOSURE THERAPY

If you want to practice exposure therapy by yourself, keep in mind that some of your fears and anxieties might elicit strong emotional or physical responses. Therefore, make sure you feel safe before you expose yourself to certain situations. It's also important to remember to go slow. Sometimes, exposure therapy can backfire on us because we've tackled something really scary without preparing ourselves for it. Therefore, it's best to go for graded exposure when trying to overcome your fears. Last but not least, you need to repeatedly expose yourself to a specific stimulus to become desensitized to it. Here are a few steps you can take to practice exposure therapy the right way:

- **Identify the fears that you want to tackle—** Make a list of the fears that you want to overcome so that you can set your goals accordingly. If possible, look out for fears that you can combine together. For example, if you have a fear of making small talk and a fear of approaching strangers, you can combine the two and try to overcome them together. Don't overdo it, however. We don't want to get overwhelmed when we have too much to handle at the same time.
- **Build your fear ladder—**Since we're going for graded exposure, you need to first construct a hierarchy of fears that you want to deal with. This means that the smaller fears go first and the ones that you're most scared to confront go in the end. You can also choose to create tiers

within each fear. What do I mean by this? For example, if your fear is related to initiating a conversation with someone, you can first decide to talk to them for only 2–3 minutes. Maybe you could ask them to give you five minutes of their time? This will usually be less intimidating than if you were to ask someone to have an hour-long discussion with you. Similarly, if you avoid going to any party, your first step can be to go to those parties where someone you know will be there and then gradually move on to those where you don't know anyone.

- **Create SMART goals to face your fears—** We've learned how to create SMART goals to overcome our anxieties. Similarly, you can create goals to tackle every fear that you have. This is the most important part because it'll ensure that you expose yourself repeatedly to the situations you normally avoid. It might take some time to understand which goals are too easy and which are too difficult. For example, it might not be reasonable to ask yourself to give a speech in front of hundreds of people in the beginning. However, you need to keep increasing the number of people you're speaking to over time. For example, you can start with 3–4 people and then go on to 10–15 people after a few months.

- **Practice**—Exposure therapy is only helpful when you keep repeating these exercises. However, don't jump steps or move too fast from one "rung" of the ladder to another. Give yourself some time to be okay with one aspect of your fear. For example, if you don't like standing in lines because you might need to ask for help from a stranger at some point, the first thing to do is to get comfortable with standing in a line. This might take some time, and it's important to be patient with it before you move on to talking to people in the line. Also, it's perfectly okay to regress at times. This means that if you think you've conquered a fear and it comes back after some time, don't beat yourself up about it.

- **Don't forget to celebrate**—Getting over a fear is a huge achievement, and you should feel proud of it. Every time you successfully do something that helps conquer yourself, reward yourself for doing so. It doesn't matter how small the gesture is; what's important is that you give yourself credit for working on yourself.

Also, if you feel that a particular fear is becoming too overwhelming for you to deal with, it's a good idea to talk to a professional about it.

REDUCING AVOIDANCE AND ADDRESSING SAFETY BEHAVIORS

We've talked about how CBT can help us think through the negative beliefs, patterns, and behaviors that we use to deal with our fears and anxieties. In this section, we'll learn to identify the different kinds of avoidance we might be indulging in. We'll also understand how we can reduce our avoidance behaviors over time.

Broadly speaking, there are five different kinds of avoidance that you might be dealing with:

- **Cognitive avoidance**—This means that you're trying not to think about something or someone who could make you anxious.
- **Situational avoidance**—Here, you might try to avoid specific situations that exacerbate your anxiety.
- **Somatic avoidance**—If you don't want your anxiety to manifest physically, you might limit yourself so that you don't sweat, tremble, or show your anxiety in obvious ways. This might

mean that you don't take part in any
stimulating, scary, or unpredictable activity.

- **Protective avoidance**—This means that you're
  spending a lot of time and energy indulging in
  safety behaviors that make you feel protected.
  For some, this could mean obsessively cleaning
  everything that they can. For others, it could
  manifest in the form of checking their
  surroundings all the time. Some others might
  feel the need to hold on to charms or totems
  that make them feel protected. The problem
  arises when we cannot function without
  performing these safety behaviors regularly.

- **Substitution avoidance**—Sometimes, you don't
  want to worry anymore. So, you might consider
  doing something else to distract yourself from
  all the anxiety. However, this is still a form of
  avoidance because you might either be
  indulging in something that's not good for you,
  or you might be using the activity to avoid
  having to deal with the actual issue.

Once you understand what kinds of behaviors you're participating in, you need to ask yourself a few questions to help you reduce these behaviors:

- How long have I been avoiding something and how long do I want to avoid it?
- How does my avoidance help me? Is there a point after which it stops being useful?
- How does my avoidance affect those around me?
- Why exactly am I avoiding this?
- Have I ever tried to confront my fears instead of avoiding the situation? If yes, how did it feel when I did that?
- What are some useful behaviors that can help me get over my fear instead of maintaining it?

You can start by tackling those behaviors that are easier to overcome and gradually move on to more difficult ones.

ROLE-PLAYING AND REHEARSAL

One of the most effective ways of dealing with your fears and anxieties is role-playing. When you role-play with someone, you enact situations that scare you and try to come up with the best ways of dealing with them.

At the same time, you know that you're not being exposed to this situation in real life, which makes it less anxiety-inducing for you. When you gain some confidence through role-plays, you can even move on to rehearsing what you've learned in real-life scenarios.

Another advantage of role-plays is that, once you're comfortable with them, you can enact them without the presence of a therapist or professional. In fact, you can even ask a friend or family member to assist you during role-plays.

Are role-plays effective? A study conducted on people who suffered from social phobia found that role-plays were as effective as medication in reducing social phobia. Also, if role-plays were done regularly, followed by real-life rehearsals, they could prove to be a cost-effective treatment for social phobia (Falloon et al., 1981).

Role-plays can help people in various ways:

- It can be used in CBT to understand how someone actually thinks or behaves when faced with a difficult situation.
- When therapists are involved, they can intervene during role-plays to help disrupt different learned patterns and behaviors.

- We can work on different responses to the same scenario until we discover something that works for us. In other words, we can experiment in a safe manner.
- Role-plays also help in practicing whatever we have learned. For example, if we've discussed using an alternative behavior when we're anxious, we can test it out through role-plays.
- Usually, we're worried about the reactions of the other person in social situations, especially if those reactions aren't pleasant. This makes us entirely avoid such situations. Through role-plays, we can prepare ourselves for their real-life versions without feeling like we're being put on the spot.

Here is how you enact a role-play with a therapist or a trustworthy individual:

- **Identify the problem or situation you want to tackle**—Be as specific as possible. Why is this situation so difficult for you? What are the challenges you face when you are in such a situation? Do you have a particular incident that started this pattern?
- **Make it as realistic as possible**—Add details to the scenario that make the situation relevant to

your life. If you have real incidents to take inspiration from, include those details as well. The more realistic the scenario, the more helpful the role-play will be.

- **Decide which role you will play**—In most cases, you'll be playing yourself, as you would want to learn how to deal with situations that are otherwise difficult for you. However, you can also try to play the role of the other person sometimes. This can be really interesting because you might get a glimpse of what it feels like to be in a conversation with you. You might even find that you don't have a lot to worry about in many cases.

- **Complete the role-play**—You can use a script to act out the scenario, or you can simply improvise as you go. This is where you can experiment with different responses and see how they make you feel.

- **Discuss with your partner**—A role-play is most successful when you have a discussion afterward with your partner. In this discussion, you can ask them whether you could have changed something or if there was something you did particularly well.

COGNITIVE BEHAVIORAL THERAPY EXERCISES FOR OVERCOMING FEAR

Exercise One

Step 1: Make a list of all the fears that you want to tackle within a period of time.

Step 2: Describe those fears in detail—making a note of your triggers and how these fears make you feel.

Step 3: Write down all the ways in which you try to avoid confronting your fears. How does it make you feel?

Step 4: Now, imagine if you could overcome these fears. What would your life look like then?

Step 5: What are the exact steps you need to take to overcome each fear? Write down at least five to six steps for each fear.

Step 6: What do you need to make these steps possible? Do you need a support group? Do you need help from someone in your life? Write them down without thinking about feasibility at this point.

Step 7: What is the most realistic next step you can take to get closer to your goals?

Exercise Two: Empty Chair Role-Play (Sutton, 2023a)

In this exercise, you will be seated on a chair, while the chair facing you will be empty. In this chair, you can imagine either a version of you or someone you need to have a conversation with being seated. This is especially helpful if the person you need to talk to isn't usually easy to have a conversation with. It makes you feel less intimidated while also letting you be honest about how they make you feel.

Usually, a therapist takes you through certain questions or scenarios as you imagine talking to the "person" in the empty chair. For example, they might ask you to tell that person about something that might have hurt you in the past. Or they might ask you to talk openly about your challenges when dealing with that person. Based on your responses, your therapist will get a sense of your innermost thoughts and beliefs regarding a scenario. Of course, you can also do this exercise with someone you trust.

Take one scenario that you would like to enact and imagine that you're behaving exactly as you would if the other person was there. See how it makes you feel. You can also enact different scenarios and see what makes you feel comfortable.

Exercise Three: Unfinished Business (Sutton, 2023a)

Sometimes, our deepest fears and anxieties are attached to conversations that we've never been able to have. In some cases, the person we wanted to talk to might not be alive. In others, they might be alive but not available to have a discussion with us. Maybe there's too much hurt to make things better between the two of you in real life. Or you might not want to interact with them ever again. However, the things left unsaid can sometimes make you scared for life.

For example, if you allowed yourself to be vulnerable with someone and they didn't respect you enough or mocked you for opening up to them, you could be worried about the same happening again. This could make you completely closed off and unable to give anyone a chance to get close to you again.

Through this exercise, you can imagine that you're talking to that person. Your therapist or a friend could play that role. Then, you can tell them exactly how you felt because of their behavior. The other person could apologize to you or at least acknowledge your feelings. Slowly—maybe through multiple sessions—you could find yourself willing to move on from the feelings of hurt and betrayal.

Now that we've conquered our fears, let's learn how to become the confident woman we all deserve to be.

6

THE CONFIDENT WOMAN

As women, we're often less confident in ourselves than we should be. We're not entirely to blame. After all, the world we live in isn't always friendly or kind to us. Sometimes, our own family members and close friends might tell us to limit ourselves. When we've grown up thinking that we must not be *too* ambitious or too confident, it can be really difficult to unlearn those lessons as adults.

In this chapter, we'll talk about why we women should be more confident in ourselves and also learn how to increase our self-esteem and self-confidence.

YOU OWN IT, GIRL!

Have you ever wondered what you bring to the table in a conversation, personal relationship, or workplace? If you do, you're not alone. Many women believe that they don't have anything great to offer others, but that's simply not true. We have a lot of strengths when it comes to communication that we should be proud of:

- Women tend to be **more empathetic** than men across ages and cultures, according to a recent study (Greenberg et al., 2022). Greater empathy means that they can understand people and their experiences even if they're not going through something similar themselves. Empathy is a great asset not only in personal relationships but also at work.
- Women tend to **form groups, find community, and collaborate with each other**. This might be because they want to feel less lonely as they navigate a world that sometimes seems governed by men. Not only that, but women are still predominantly the caregivers in their families. So, they need to rely on each other to deal with the challenges and share the joys that come with such roles. As we've seen in the recent past, communities are absolutely

essential for society to sustain itself during challenging times.

- We've all heard about the famed "**women's intuition,**" which allows us to sense things that aren't obvious. In general, we tend to focus on the smaller details that others might have missed. Not only do we understand people better, but we can also read the room and communicate accordingly if needed.

- Women are usually **more emotionally intelligent** than men. In fact, a study found that women perform better than men in 11 out of 12 emotional intelligence skills (*The female "soft skills" that can boost workplace success, 2020*).

So, if you're a woman, your soft skills are already a boon to yourself and others. What you need is to believe in yourself and in your worth.

HOW TO BE MORE CONFIDENT

Confidence isn't something you're born with. So, stop telling yourself that it's too late for you to build confidence.

Here are some things you can do to become more confident over time:

- **Pay attention to your body language**—Before you appear confident to others, you need to feel confident within yourself. You might not even notice it, but the way you carry yourself has a lot of impact on how you feel. For example, if you're not feeling confident in yourself, you might assume a crouched position. Or you might have a tendency to walk with your eyes on the ground. So, first, look into the mirror and see what needs to be changed. Consciously hold your head up high when you walk, assume a good posture while sitting or standing, and dress smartly. You don't have to wear anything expensive as long as you feel confident in it.
- **Push yourself to go outside your comfort zone**—Many of us think that we need a certain level of confidence to try something new. In fact, we often say things like, "That could never be me," or "I wonder where they get the courage to do this." The truth is courage follows courage. Meaning you need to take the first step even if you're afraid. Once you start doing things that you don't normally do, you'll begin to find the courage to do other things like that.

- **Learn to appreciate yourself for every little thing**—How many times have you held back on praising yourself because you thought you hadn't done anything "worthy" enough? Sometimes, we're made to feel bad about feeling proud of ourselves. Don't fall into the trap. Life is hard, and some days you earn points simply for trying your best. Confidence comes from knowing you're worth it *all the time.*

- **Have faith in your purpose**—Sometimes, we don't feel confident about something simply because we don't know why we're doing it. For example, if you're following someone else's dream, it can be very difficult to have faith in yourself when the going gets tough. However, when we know who we are and what we're trying to achieve, we can be confident even when others try to pull us down.

- **Speak up every now and then**—Many of us think that if we keep our opinions to ourselves and agree with others, we can come across as more agreeable people. Of course, there's an implicit expectation from women to always be agreeable. Now, I'm not saying that you need to become combative and refute everything that is being said. However, you need to work on speaking up more often, especially when you think your opinion could add something of value to a discussion. Remember, it's not inherently wrong to hold a different view from the majority. In fact, it can even help in adding a new dimension to a topic that no one else has thought of. I know that you might face backlash when you start voicing your opinions, but don't let that deter you. The more you start speaking up, the more confidence you'll gain over time.

- **Are you your worst enemy?**—When we grow up hearing all the different reasons why women should not be assertive or why they should act in a certain way, we internalize some of these messages. Sometimes, we might not even realize that we're holding to certain stereotypes just to make ourselves feel safe and accepted among others. The next time you find yourself saying, "Who do I think I am to dream so big?" counter it with, "Who's told me that I cannot dream big?" Check your own assumptions about your capabilities.

- **Get comfortable with being wrong every now and then**—Have you ever felt shaken when you were wrong about something and then sworn to yourself that you will never try again? As it turns out, society places a lot of pressure on women to be "perfect." We need to be flawless to be loved and accepted; otherwise, we're worth nothing. Well, not only is perfection an illusion, but the perfect woman is a construct that keeps us from being our amazing selves. It might take some time for society to catch up, but we can certainly tell ourselves that it's okay to mess up every now and then. In fact, mistakes are how we learn and gain confidence to do better next time.

SELF-COMPASSION IS KEY

Why do we need self-compassion? Professor and author Kristin Neff published a book called *Fierce Self-Compassion* in 2021. What is fierce self-compassion, and what does it ask of us?

In a world that often tells us to keep quiet and follow arbitrary rules set by the patriarchy, it's normal to feel frustrated, angry, and helpless at the same time. Through fierce self-compassion, we want to reinvent the narrative and take back control of our lives. We pay attention to any injustice meted out to us, we fight for our rights, and we give ourselves the space to love without asking for anyone else's permission. While anger is a necessary emotion in some cases, we cannot survive and win this battle on anger alone. We also need to be kind to ourselves and offer ourselves the compassion that this world sometimes denies us.

What Are the Steps to Fierce Self-Compassion?

Here is what you can do to become more compassionate toward yourself:

- **Be honest about how you feel at any time—** Don't pretend to be okay when you're not. If something affects you deeply—especially in a negative manner—don't dismiss it just because others do. At the same time, be mindful about not losing yourself in the emotion. For example, you can acknowledge that you're feeling angry without letting it unsettle you completely.
- **Remind yourself that you're not alone—** Weirdly enough, self-pity and self-compassion don't go together. So, even though you might feel like you're the only one going through something difficult, remember that this is not true. Recognizing your struggles as being shared by others can make you feel better.
- **Ask yourself what you need in the moment—** What is the best way for you to take care of yourself right now? Even if it's something you

cannot give yourself right now, acknowledge it and look for the next best solution.

- **Place a hand on your heart**—This simple gesture can let you feel more connected to yourself. If you want, you can place your hand flat against your heart, or you can even make a fist and place it gently on your heart. When you make a fist, you're giving yourself both courage and heart to go on.

- **Forgive yourself for not showing up for yourself**—You'll not always be able to stand up for yourself. There will be days when you'll be too tired to even try. That's okay. Life gets the better of us sometimes. During these moments, you need to love yourself extra hard.

BUILDING SELF-ESTEEM AND SELF-WORTH

A person who has self-esteem will acknowledge their qualities and know that they are worthy of being loved and respected all the time. Ironically, our self-esteem is challenged more when we step out into the world. When we're repeatedly told that we're not good enough, we start believing others instead of tuning into our own inner voice.

How do you rebuild your self-worth? Here are some things you can try:

- **Focus on your best qualities**—Better still, write down everything you think is amazing about you. If you feel like you don't have much to say about yourself, ask your loved ones to do so. Make sure that you don't listen to people who give you backhanded compliments or always add a negative comment to a positive one—just to even things out (we all know someone like this!).

- **Don't compare yourself to others**—Nothing kills self-esteem faster than seeing someone else's life and blaming yourself for not living it. Remember that self-esteem is about you, not about someone else. If you keep looking for happiness in other people's lives, not only will you never find it, but you'll also lose sight of what you do have.

- **Tell yourself that you're not defined by your looks, job, or status**—I know how hard this can be. Everywhere we look, people seem to be chasing these things because it's the only way to mean something in this world. However, this is not true. Your worth isn't determined by anything that's external to you. Who are you without these things? Who are you in love? Who are you in solitude? Who are you when no one's watching and when there are no consequences for your actions? Familiarize yourself with that person because that's your true self. Our true selves are always worthy.

- **Practice being your own cheerleader**—Don't get me wrong. All of us need to rely on others every now and then. Our lives are richer for the people who love us and encourage us to be our best selves. However, when we start depending on others to validate us, it can become really difficult to show up for ourselves when no one's around. Every so often, we'll need to do things and make decisions completely on our own. So, it's best to learn how to become our own cheerleader.

How To Be Your Own Cheerleader

Here are some steps that you can follow:

- **Schedule some one-on-one time with yourself**—If we spend a lot of time with others, we might forget how enjoyable our own company is. If you're not particularly social, you might limit yourself to activities in the house. While that is great, you should also try to have fun all by yourself, preferably in the outer world. If you don't like going out too much, start with the small things. Walk to the nearest grocery store once a week and spend some time walking through the aisles. Schedule a day of pampering yourself without making plans with your best friend. This won't be fun in the beginning, but you're going to start enjoying yourself sooner than you think. This way, you'll be less reliant on others to have a good time or to navigate this world.

- **Affirmations to the rescue**—It might seem cheesy or goofy when you start giving compliments to the person in the mirror, but it'll do you a world of good. Write down a few things about yourself that you want to repeat regularly. You don't have to be insincere; in fact, these work best when you believe in them. For example, if you've always heard that you're not pretty, take some time to think about the features you like. Maybe you've got a beautiful smile or you've got lovely eyes. Pay close attention to yourself—not with a critical eye but with love—and you'll find a lot of good things about yourself.

- **Remember that acceptance and self-love take time**—If you're a perfectionist, or if you get impatient with yourself, you might find it difficult to stay on this journey. What's important is that you show up each day and stay committed to the process.

HOW TO BECOME MORE ASSERTIVE

In general, women have trouble being assertive in their lives. This could be because they've been taught to be "pleasant" at all times. Women with low self-esteem usually believe that they don't have the right to establish boundaries with others. However, being assertive is a skill that teaches us to be confident about what we need and ask others to acknowledge our needs.

Here are some tips to become more assertive with people in your life:

- **Establish boundaries early**—Often, we wait too long to communicate our boundaries to other people, especially in personal relationships. We might not want to hurt the other person or make them feel less valued, which is why we think it's best to play along as long as possible. It's much easier, however, to establish boundaries early on in the relationship.

- **Practice saying no without disrespecting people**—When we go from being passive to assertive all of a sudden, we might accidentally become aggressive in the process. Remember, if you need to put down others or be aggressive to get your point across, you either don't have a solid argument or you lack confidence in yourself. So, check your tone and other nonverbal cues when you're saying "no."

- **Identify certain areas of your life where you want to establish healthy boundaries**—Do you want more time to yourself at home? Do you want to reduce the number of times you meet friends? Do you want work that is better suited to your qualifications and interests? Focus on one area and start saying "no" at least once a week to begin with. It will likely not be pleasant for both you and the other person, especially if they're used to you saying "yes" all the time. However, don't let the discomfort scare you. Over time, you'll become more confident in saying no when needed.

- **Use "I" statements whenever you want to assert yourself**—Make sure that your statement is about how you feel rather than how someone else makes you feel. When you talk about your feelings or needs, you're acknowledging yourself without diminishing the other person. However, when you start saying "you" all the time, you might make the person feel targeted and even misunderstood.

- **Prioritize the right relationships in your life** —This is extremely difficult to learn and implement, especially for women. This is because we spend most of our lives trying to take care of others or please others. This can erode our sense of self and we can spend our lives doubting our own instincts. Remember that our relationships should energize us. If certain interactions always leave you drained, confused, and unsure of yourself, you're better off without such relationships in your life. Once you cut out these toxic voices from your life, you might be surprised at how kind your own voice is. Also, be aware of the fact that you might end up losing people in this process. Once you start asserting yourself, people who cannot use you in any way might distance themselves from you. While this can be difficult in the short run, know that you're better off without them in the long run.

EXERCISE TO BUILD YOUR SELF-ESTEEM

Seeing Yourself For Who You Are

In this exercise, you'll challenge all the negative thoughts you have about yourself by replacing them with positive ones.

First, you need to make a list of all the things you might have heard from others or that you have told yourself over the years. Put them into two categories—positive and negative. Chances are, the list of negatives will be longer than the list of positives.

Second, you need to start questioning all the negative things that you've been taking for granted all this time. For example, if you think you're not fun, take some time and think about all the times when you *were* fun. Think hard because you might have repressed many of the good things about yourself without realizing it. Ask the people that you love if they can help you challenge these beliefs. Now, you might not want to believe them because they love you. So, ask them for specific examples. Now, write these down and go through them.

Third, write down all the positive things about you in the form of affirmations on Post-it notes and stick them in places that you frequent. These could include your bathroom mirror, the desk at which you work, and or even on your pillow. Remind yourself constantly about everything that makes you amazing.

EXERCISE TO BUILD YOUR CONFIDENCE

Learning to Say No

Step 1: Think of common scenarios where you might have adopted an extremely passive or aggressive stance.

Step 2: Why did you do so? Why did you think that it was better to keep quiet or to be rude to someone? Keep asking yourself questions till you uncover the reason behind your behavior.

Step 3: Prepare a script or make a list of things to keep in mind when you're presented with a similar scenario in the future.

Step 4: After you say no to someone, write down your experiences and feelings during the process. How did you say no? What was their reaction? How did you feel after you said no to them? Are there any lingering feelings of discomfort or embarrassment? Do you think you could have said the same thing in a different way? Do you feel more confident saying no in the future?

Step 5: Pay attention to any tendencies of over-apologizing while saying no. You're entitled to make decisions that work for you. Instead of saying, "I'm so sorry for not being able to attend this event with you," you can say, "I'm looking forward to the next time we attend something together."

Now that we've learned how to become confident, let's arm ourselves with some much-needed social skills.

7

BEING SOCIALLY ARMED

I n this chapter, we'll learn how to build our social skills. We'll understand the importance of effective communication, active listening, and small talk and also learn how to maintain healthy relationships.

THE IMPORTANCE OF EFFECTIVE COMMUNICATION

Here are some ways in which effective communication helps us:

- **It can help reduce or resolve conflict with others**—Conflicts occur when we're not on the same page with someone else. This could be because we've misunderstood what they've said or because we're not listening to them. Sometimes, it might simply be a case of good old-fashioned confusion. However, there's almost nothing that honest and transparent communication can't solve.

- **It helps build trust in our relationships—** When we communicate effectively with people, we let them know who we truly are. When we deal with criticism or resolve conflicts without becoming angry, we tell them that we're committed to our relationship with them. Even when things are tough, and especially then, effective communication makes people trust others and work together.

- **It helps build engagement at work—**When we communicate effectively at work, especially if we're in a leadership position, we help others feel appreciated and seen. People who know what is expected of them at all times and who also know that they can approach someone when they're having issues tend to give more of themselves at work. They're more motivated, more connected with others, and they feel a greater sense of purpose at work. All of this helps in building employee engagement.

- **Good communication makes us feel like we're all on the same team—**This is true of both personal and professional relationships. Poor communication can make you feel like you're always engaged in a battle to make someone else understand you. Effective communication, on the other hand, can make you feel like you're both fighting for the same cause.

HOW TO BECOME AN EFFECTIVE COMMUNICATOR

Here are some tips that can help you become an effective communicator:

- **Know yourself, your audience, and your content**—Even before you communicate with someone, you should know why you're doing so. Of course, not every conversation needs prior preparation, but you should still have a sense of what you bring to the table when you talk to someone. Being generally well-read also helps because you're not left scrambling for topics when you meet someone unexpectedly. Knowing our audience also helps because we know what we can and cannot say to them. You can prepare the best speech in the world but it'll fall flat if it's not a good fit for your audience.

Also, the more prepared you are, the more confident you'll feel while talking to others.

- **Pay attention to clarity and speed while talking**—If you're not prepared, or if you're too nervous, you might end up speaking too fast or jumble up your words. When you feel anxious, try to consciously slow down and emphasize your words. Also, it's a good idea not to over-rehearse or to memorize a script when you're talking. Otherwise, you might find yourself getting even more nervous if you forget something, and the script might make your speech seem less natural.

- **Timing is extremely important**—No matter how amazing you are as a speaker or how much preparation you've done, you might still mess up things if the timing is not right. For example, if you're approaching someone who seems busy or preoccupied, they'll likely be irritated about the intrusion and not pay enough attention to what you have to say. Similarly, if your partner is tired after a long day and you start complaining as soon as they enter the house, they might not be receptive to your points, even if they're valid.

- **Pay attention to what you're not saying**— Your words are important but so is your body language. In fact, your body language might convey more about you than you think. If you're prone to getting anxious every now and then, your body might communicate that to others. For example, your tone or pitch might change, your body might become tense, or you might struggle to make eye contact with people. Sometimes, when you're feeling particularly anxious, you might even give others the impression of being unapproachable. This might make them think that you're not interested in talking to them. So, work on your nonverbal cues just as much as you work on your verbal communication.

- **Practice active listening**—If you think effective communication is all about talking, think again. Most effective communicators know how to listen to others. As difficult as it is to learn how to speak well, it's even more difficult to become an active listener.

PRACTICING ACTIVE LISTENING

There are many kinds of listening that we engage in on a regular basis. For example, we listen to music to relax ourselves and to feel good. Similarly, we listen to podcasts so that we can learn something new and keep ourselves informed and entertained at the same time. Sometimes, we listen only to decide how best to refute what they're saying. This could be done during a formal or informal debate. If you spend some time on social media, you'll likely find yourself in the midst of such debates. Most people aren't really interested in listening to what others have to say. They're more interested in what they have to say in response.

There is only one kind of listening where we want to understand another person's point of view. This is known as empathic listening. Even if we don't know what they're talking about, or if we have a different opinion from theirs, we still want to hear what they have to say. We're not doing this to prove a point to ourselves or to corroborate our own views about a topic but to see things from their perspective. Active listening is a part of empathic listening.

Active listening implies that the person talking deserves all your attention and respect. It also means that you're willing to engage with them in a way that doesn't dismiss them. Most of us think we're giving someone our attention, but we're usually busy thinking about the important project that we're engaged in or what we'll be having for dinner tonight. Sometimes, it's not completely our fault as the speaker might not be "engaging" us. Still, when we don't pay attention to others, we undermine the conversation and miss out on the chance to connect with someone.

Let's discuss some tips that can help us become active listeners:

- **Make sure you're paying attention to them at all times**—If you're distracted by something, leave your distractions at the door. Keep your devices on silent, and don't attend to any calls or texts until the conversation is over.

- **Show the speaker that you're interested in listening to them**—Simple body language cues can let the speaker know that you're listening to them. For example, when you tilt your head slightly, you convey interest. Similarly, when you're not fidgety, you're telling them that you want to be there. Try to maintain gentle eye contact with them. Don't stare at them in such a way that they become uncomfortable, but let them know that you're listening intently to them.

- **Pay attention to their body language and try mirroring it**—When you're truly listening to someone, your body language begins to mirror them. Of course, it shouldn't look weird or exaggerated. If their body language conveys anxiety or lack of confidence, try to encourage them through non-verbal cues like nodding or smiling (if appropriate).

- **As much as possible, try not to interrupt the speaker**—Maybe they're saying something that you agree with or you want to add something to what they're saying. As tempting as it might be, don't interrupt them while they're speaking. Instead, make a note of the things that you might like to discuss with them later.

- **Try not to judge or come to immediate conclusions**—These days, we're all under pressure to form opinions as soon as possible. However, this isn't helpful when you're trying to understand someone. If what they're saying is very different from your point of view, keep an open mind and listen to why they believe what they do. Also, don't be in a hurry to summarize their speech.

- **Don't start framing your own response while they're still talking**—In fact, don't respond immediately after they've finished either. Make sure that they've said everything they need to say. You can even repeat what they've said to let them know that you're listening to them. Make sure you understand them before you give them an answer.

- **Ask questions where relevant**—If you don't understand or want further clarity on something, ask questions. Try to keep them as open-ended as possible so that there's room for exploration.

LEARNING THE ART OF SMALL TALK

If you feel like you're terrible at small talk, you're not alone. Many people struggle with small talk, especially because you need to maintain a balance between being breezy and still making an impact. Most people don't like small talk because it can seem like you're talking about "nothing really," but small talk is an effective way to break the ice when you don't know someone.

Here are some ways in which you can be effective at small talk:

- **Think about a few topics that you can discuss with anyone**—Make sure that these topics aren't controversial in nature or related to religion, politics, or anything that can polarize people.
- **If you don't know how to start with small talk, you can always start with a question**— This can be a simple question that most people

will have an answer to, but the question should be open-ended in nature.

- **Listen carefully to whatever the other people are saying**—You might chance upon a topic that you can talk about, or you might realize that you have an interesting perspective to share.

- **Use humor if possible**—Humor is tricky as it can end up offending people or falling flat, but if used well, it's the easiest way to get people to open up to you. It's best to be observant about your surroundings and make a light-hearted remark that doesn't disrespect anyone. In fact, if you're a socially awkward person, you can even joke about yourself.

- **Look for ways to connect with people**— Wherever possible, look for common interests or something that you share with others. People warm up to those they think are similar to them in some way.

BUILDING AND MAINTAINING HEALTHY RELATIONSHIPS THROUGH COMMUNICATION

Here are some ways in which you can build great relationships with others:

- **Have a good relationship with yourself**—If you don't know who you are, what you want from a relationship, and what you can give to others—you'll struggle to build and maintain healthy relationships with other people. As counterintuitive as it might seem, you need to spend time with yourself and get to know yourself before expecting anything from your relationships.
- **Be willing to make an effort**—Sometimes, popular media makes it seem like relationships are all about luck and magic. However, most healthy relationships survive on hard work. I am not saying that you cannot have fun in your relationships. In fact, if maintaining a relationship seems like too much work, you're probably in the wrong relationship. Instead, you should be more than willing to put in the required effort for a relationship to thrive.

- **Respect your own and others' boundaries—** There are different reasons why boundaries might become hazy in relationships. At work, you might have someone who disrespects other people's boundaries all the time. In personal relationships, you might think that boundaries imply a lack of love. However, boundaries are extremely important for any relationship to thrive. If you want others to respect your boundaries, make sure that you're respecting theirs.

- **Apologize without letting your ego get in the way—**Don't be too concerned about being right in an argument. As long as you're not fighting over an ideological issue, you should not let ego get in the way of your relationships. If you're wrong, don't hesitate to apologize to the other person. Even if you don't think you're wrong, don't obsess over proving yourself right when it comes to minor disagreements. Show the other person that the relationship you have with them takes precedence over everything else.

- **Learn about the other person's communication style—**Sometimes, the only issue between two people is that they communicate in vastly different ways. For example, someone might have a habit of finding humor in everything, while the other person might be more sincere. Similarly, someone might want to resolve conflicts as soon as possible, while the other person might want to take some time before they discuss anything. If possible, try to understand how the other person communicates and what they need from you as well. You might not be able to change everything, but being aware of the differences between you can certainly help.

EXERCISES FOR EFFECTIVE COMMUNICATION

Exercise One: Getting to Know Each Other

This is an interesting exercise. For this, you don't need to talk to a stranger or to someone you barely know. In fact, go ahead and choose someone you're really close to for this one. Prepare a set of questions that you would like to ask them. Ask them to do the same for you. Then, write down what you think will be their answers to these questions. When you're done, exchange your answer sheets and check how many of their answers are correct. You might be surprised to know how well you know each other or that you still don't know many things about the other person. Another version of this exercise involves telling the other person stories about your life that might surprise them.

Exercise Two: Active Listening Reflection

One of the ways of getting better at active listening is by reflecting on how you performed during a conversation. Through this exercise, you can assess which areas you're good in and which require improvement.

Answer the following questions honestly:

- How many times did you check your phone, watch, or the door during the conversation?
- Were you paying attention to others in the room, or were you only paying attention to the speaker?
- Did you make a note of things you found interesting, or were you constantly interrupting the speaker?
- What was your body language like? Was your posture correct? Did you show them that you were interested? Did you maintain eye contact? Was your posture open or closed?
- Did you encourage them with nonverbal cues or words that convey interest?

- Did you use open-ended questions to gain a deeper understanding of the topic?
- Were you able to repeat some of what the speaker was talking about to let them know that you're interested or that you have certain doubts?
- Did the speaker seem satisfied or encouraged after their speech? Were they eager to talk to you again?
- How did you feel after the conversation? Did you feel like you learned something and/or made a great connection with the speaker?

EXERCISE FOR MAINTAINING HEALTHY RELATIONSHIPS

Exercise One: Dealing With Conflicts in a Healthy Manner

If you're someone who gets jittery at the thought of conflicts, you might need some help in peacefully resolving them without letting them overwhelm you.

Step 1: Check in with yourself. Are you in a calm mood and willing to listen to the other person? If yes, then move to step two; otherwise, give yourself some time to be ready.

Step 2: Check in with the person you're in a conflict with. Is this a good time for them? Do they need more time? If they're ready, move on to the next step.

Step 3: Calmly let them know your side of the story. Try not to get emotional while doing so, as it can derail the conversation and unsettle both of you.

Step 4: Ask them to let you know what their arguments are.

Step 5: While they're talking, try to apply active listening techniques to understand where they're coming from.

Step 6: Don't dismiss their concerns even if you think that they're exaggerated. Let them know that you hear them.

Step 7: Take accountability for your part in the conflict. Acknowledge your mistakes without sounding defensive or saying statements like, "I know I did this but you did that."

Step 8: Ask them if they want to come up with solutions together. Be honest about the aspects of the conflict that can be resolved and those that cannot be. Come up with an action plan that could help resolve the conflict in a certain amount of time. Agree to disagree on certain aspects of the conflict.

Step 9: Ask the other person if they want to schedule regular check-ins to make sure that minor issues don't snowball into major conflicts in the future.

Now that we've discussed how to become an effective communicator, let's make sure we cement these wins.

8

MORE TIPS FOR TRANSITIONING TO A SOCIAL BUTTERFLY

I n the last chapter, we'll discuss some tips that will help us keep our social anxiety at bay and become effective communicators.

STRATEGIES FOR OVERCOMING SETBACKS AND STAYING MOTIVATED

The path to becoming an effective communicator and overcoming our social anxiety isn't a linear one. There will be days when we feel defeated and days when we feel like we've regressed. The first thing to remember is that everyone has these days.

That being said, there are some things you can do to keep yourself motivated during this period:

- **Don't dwell on your mistakes**—While it's important to learn from your mistakes, constantly thinking about them doesn't help you in any way. Acknowledge what happened and move on.
- **Remind yourself why you started this journey**—You always knew this was going to be tough, right? What was the reason behind embarking on this journey in the first place? What was your purpose? Remind yourself why you can't give up.
- **Take some time off**—It's okay to want some time off before you start again. During this time, don't guilt yourself into doing anything you don't want to. Shower yourself with love and care before you take the plunge once more.
- **Pay attention to what went wrong the last time and make changes**—You would likely have set some goals and made plans when you started this journey. However, you should also be flexible about making changes if something is not working for you. Accept that this is a journey where you need to experiment, fail, and learn all the time.

- **Focus on taking one step each day**—I know I talked about taking the plunge but I didn't mean that you need to overwhelm yourself when you return. Promise yourself that you'll do one thing that brings you closer to your goals each day.
- **Find your people**—Failure hurts, and it hurts terribly. It can also seem extremely isolating. During this time, if you don't have people who understand and encourage you, you might take longer to bounce back. So, surround yourself with people who understand that failure is a part of the process but it's equally important to get up after some time.

THE IMPORTANCE OF FOLLOWING YOUR PASSIONS

While it's important to find meaning in what you do, it's also important to know what gives your life meaning. How do you find out what you're passionate about? Well, what is something that you would do even if no one paid you for it? What is something you can talk about for hours on end? What is something that perks you up when you're tired? What is something that doesn't feel like work? Answer these questions honestly and you'll figure out your passion. You might have more than one passion (lucky you!), and you might not even want to monetize your passion. The important thing is to keep space in your life for these passions.

When you follow your passions, you learn courage. You also understand the value of persisting at something because it means a lot to you. Not only will you feel creatively stimulated, but you'll also be able to take calculated risks over time. Passion gives purpose to your life, which means that you might feel more motivated and confident on a daily basis. This confidence can affect different areas of your life and make you feel less anxious as a result.

A LITTLE IMPULSIVITY ALSO WORKS

When you think of impulsive behavior, you might think that it's undesirable. After all, being impulsive often leads to poor decision-making and lots of unpleasant consequences for everyone involved. People who make impulsive decisions are seen as rash or insensitive. However, these views have been challenged in the last few years. For example, a study showed that "impulsive" behaviors can also be strategic, meaning that they're not always devoid of thought or consideration (Kopetz et al., 2018).

One aspect of impulsive behavior—known as "functional impulsivity"—can also be useful to us. For example, impulsive thinking could help generate new ideas without worrying about whether those ideas are "good enough." This is why many artists and writers swear by the idea of creating impulsively. Also, those of us who spend a lot of time ruminating and overthinking might benefit from being impulsive from time to time.

What does it mean for people who're usually anxious about everything they do? For example, those of us who keep thinking for days about the possible consequences of initiating a conversation with a stranger might do well to be impulsive every now and then. Maybe if we didn't always think about what *could* happen, we would be able to make things happen by putting ourselves out there and grabbing opportunities to connect with others.

It's important to find balance and not use impulsivity as an excuse to be irresponsible, but there's no harm in letting impulsivity win every so often.

BUILDING YOUR SUPPORT NETWORK

Social anxiety can make you feel lonely. What's worse is that it can feel like a self-imposed prison. So, why not build your own group of people to rely on? Why not create a group that makes you feel less lonely and misunderstood? A support network doesn't mean that you don't show up for yourself or carve your own path. It simply means that you don't have to figure everything out by yourself. When you choose the people you want around you, you feel more in control of your life.

Here are some things to keep in mind while building your support network:

- **Think about the people who are already in your life**—This could include your friends, family members, mentors, and anyone who has influenced your life positively. Are they present for you? Do they have the time or energy to support you? What are their strengths? Are there any challenges in asking them for support?
- **Think about what you bring to the table**— Support is a two-way street. If you don't offer support to others, you'll have trouble sustaining these relationships for a long time. What are some of the qualities that could help you support others? Are you empathetic? Do you refrain from judging people? Can you help people with certain skills?
- **What are the different kinds of support that you need?**—No one can provide you with

everything you need. It's more likely that some people will help you in one aspect while others will offer you a different kind of support. For example, some people can offer emotional support while others can help in more practical ways. For example, many of us have that friend who can listen to us talk for hours on end—being the best listener possible. That friend makes us feel loved, validated, and safe. Then there is the friend who will take care of everything when we feel sick—they'll buy us groceries, cook food for us, and take us to the doctor. We need both kinds of friends. Similarly, we need different people for a good support group.

- **Once you know what you need, try to find it yourself**—This is the part that needs a little courage. If you want to build a support network, you need to network with others. For that, you can look for various activities that happen in your community. You can even look for online communities as long as you know they're safe and vetted. When you meet people during meetings, initiate conversations with them. You already share something in common with them, so you can use that as a starting point for your conversations. Once you're comfortable with them, ask them if they could be a part of your support network.

- **Keep checking in with your network**—Make sure that you don't reach out only when you need someone. You should also be making sure that they're doing okay. Remember that providing support and caring for people is as rewarding as it is challenging. It can get pretty overwhelming every now and then. So, make sure that the people who care for you are also taking care of themselves.

EXERCISES FOR SELF-CARE

Exercise One: What Do I Need?

In this exercise, we will look at the different aspects of self-care.

Step 1: What does physical self-care look like to me? This can include food, exercise, activities, sleep, rest, and so on.

Step 2: What does mental self-care look like to me? Am I taking care of my thinking patterns? Am I getting exhausted from all the thinking that I do? Are my thoughts helping or hindering me?

Step 3: What does emotional self-care look like to me? Am I acknowledging my emotions, no matter how difficult they might be? Am I giving myself time to process my emotions? Do I often dismiss my emotions or let others dismiss them?

Step 4: What does spiritual self-care look like to me? Is my spirit nourished? What does a healthy spiritual life feel like? Do I want to spend more time in nature? Do I want to meditate more? Do I want to read more about things that nourish my soul? Do I want to know myself on a deeper level?

Step 5: What about self-care in relationships? Am I prioritizing myself in my relationships? Do I voice my needs and concerns to people close to me? Do I keep quiet to "maintain the peace" but end up feeling resentful toward the other person? Do I feel safe and loved in my relationships? Am I compromising on certain core values to appease someone?

Write down everything that might be missing from your life in each of these categories. Think about some concrete steps you can take to bridge the gap. Set SMART goals and track your progress over time.

Exercise Two: Journaling Prompts to Help Kickstart Your Self-Care Journey

We've previously talked about the benefits of journaling to help us understand and break our negative thinking patterns and to develop self-awareness. Journaling is an amazing activity that can help you know yourself on a deeper level. It can also help you be honest with yourself without fear of judgment from others. So, here are a few questions or prompts to get you started:

- Think about the happiest moments in your life. What were they and why did they make you happy?
- What were the most challenging moments in your life? What made them so challenging?
- If money was not an issue, what would you most love doing?
- What scares you the most and why? Have you ever tried overcoming these fears? Why or why not?
- Who are your favorite people in the world? Why are they your favorites?
- What is something you admire in someone? Or what is the one trait that you wish you had?
- What are your biggest regrets in life? If you had the ability to change your past, what would you do differently?

- What are a few things that make you smile during a hard day?
- What can you do for others to make them feel better about themselves?
- What are some of the qualities that you're proud of?
- What is something that used to scare you earlier but you've overcome? How did you go about doing this?
- What does your ideal day look like? What is standing in the way of making it a reality?
- What is your favorite place, animal, or thing that can calm you down?

These are only some of the prompts that you can use to understand yourself better. They can also help give you ideas about achieving some of your goals.

CONCLUSION

Many times, an author starts writing a book when they want to give voice to their despair or frustration. They want others in similar situations to feel less lonely. To an extent, that was true for me too. However, my main reason was almost entirely opposite to this. I decided to write this book when I realized how different life could be. I had seen what was possible once I stopped letting my social anxiety dictate my life. I had experienced life in all its fullness. It seemed almost criminal that some of us could be kept away from this life simply because we didn't know what was possible.

Through this book, I want every woman to realize that the world, while unpredictable, doesn't have to be scary and anxiety-inducing. I want women to have faith in themselves and to understand that the key to unlocking this amazing world lies within them.

Here are some of the key topics that I've tried to tackle in this book:

- We understood the causes, symptoms, and effects of anxiety. We also understood the different kinds of anxiety that plague people. Then, we discussed social anxiety disorder on a deeper level through its cognitive model and physiological symptoms.
- We looked at why social anxiety affects more women than men. We explored the various factors that could contribute to social anxiety in women, including genetics, environment, hormones, and social factors.
- Then we understood how CBT can help us in overcoming our negative thoughts and behaviors and make us overcome our anxiety. We discussed various CBT methods that can be applied to help us deal with social anxiety.
- Following that, we explored the differences between shyness and social anxiety. We learned to cope with our panic attacks and to learn emotional regulation during difficult times.
- We discussed how fear can hold us back as women and how we can overcome our fears

through various methods such as exposure therapy, role-playing, and rehearsal.

- Then we talked about the lack of confidence that most women suffer from and how it affects our professional, personal, and social lives. We discussed how to cultivate self-compassion, self-esteem, and self-worth in order to become more confident in life. We also explored how women can become more assertive in their daily lives and interactions.

- After discussing confidence, we moved on to acquiring important social skills that will help us get over our social anxiety. These skills include effective communication, active listening, making small talk, and learning to build our relationships through communication.

- In the last chapter, we talked about facing challenges on this journey and overcoming any setbacks we might face from time to time. We also talked about how following our passion and being a little impulsive can help us gain more confidence in our lives and social interactions. In the end, we also discussed the importance of building our own support network that will help us when we feel anxious or intimidated in life.

I've also added certain exercises at the end of most chapters so that you can begin to put everything into practice without any delay. No matter how much you read up on these topics, you'll only begin to gain confidence when you start applying them in your daily practice. I hope these exercises inspire you to come up with certain ideas of your own.

Even though we're talking about social anxiety, this journey is extremely personal to each one of you. It's about understanding your deepest self, extending your love and compassion to it, and allowing it to have faith in itself again. It's also about challenging everything you've ever known to be true about yourself to find a version of you who is bold, adventurous, and passionate. Ultimately, it's about allowing yourself to connect deeply with the world and those living in it.

I hope this book has given you a glimpse into the kind of life that you can lead if you only believe in yourself. In the end, I would like to ask that if this book has inspired you to take a step in a new direction, please consider leaving a review on Amazon so that others might also find this book and get the help they need. I wish you all the very best on your journey.

REFERENCES

Ackerman, C. E. (2023a). *21 emotion regulation worksheets & strategies.* Positive Psychology. https://positivepsy chology.com/emotion-regulation-worksheets-strate gies-dbt-skills/#strategies-emotion-regulation

Ackerman, C. E. (2023b). *15 best self-esteem worksheets and activities.* Positive Psychology. https://positivepsy chology.com/self-esteem-worksheets/#adults-self-esteem

Alhanati, J. (2022). *Follow your passions, and success will follow.* Investopedia. https://www.investopedia.com/articles/pf/12/passion-success.asp

Anderson, A. (2021, November 22). *9 steps to mastering the art of small talk.* The British School of Excellence.

https://thebritishschoolofexcellence.com/life-skills/9-steps-to-mastering-the-art-of-small-talk/

Anthony. (2021). *Difference between shyness and social anxiety.* Mind My Peelings. https://www.mindmypeel ings.com/blog/introvert-shy-social-anxiety#:~:text=Although%20the%20symp-toms%20of%20both,level%20of%20avoidance

Anxiety. (n.d.-a). American Psychological Association. https://www.apa.org/topics/anxiety

Anxiety. (n.d.-b). NHS Inform. https://www.nhsin form.scot/illnesses-and-conditions/mental-health/anxiety

Anxiety disorders. (n.d.). Cleveland Clinic. https://my.clevelandclinic.org/health/diseases/9536-anxiety-disorders

Anxiety disorders - Symptoms and causes - Mayo Clinic. (2018, May 4). Mayo Clinic. https://www.mayoclinic.org/diseases-conditions/anxiety/symptoms-causes/syc-20350961

Anxiety signs and symptoms. (n.d.). Mind. https://www.mind.org.uk/information-support/types-of-mental-health-problems/anxiety-and-panic-attacks/symptoms/

Arabi, S. (2022, May 25). *The self-confidence formula for women*. Psych Central. https://psychcentral.com/lib/the-self-confidence-formula-for-women

Arocho, J. (2021, July 26). *How to overcome the fear of blushing*. Manhattan Center for Cognitive Behavioral Therapy. https://www.manhattancbt.com/archives/5360/fear-of-blushing/

Asher, M., & Aderka, I. M. (2018). Gender differences in social anxiety disorder. *Journal of Clinical Psychology*, *74*(10), 1730–1741. https://doi.org/10.1002/jclp.22624

Asher, M., Asnaani, A., & Aderka, I. M. (2017). Gender differences in social anxiety disorder: A review. *Clinical Psychology Review*, *56*, 1–12. https://doi.org/10.1016/j.cpr.2017.05.004

Assertiveness skills: Definition, examples and tips. (2023a). Indeed. https://www.indeed.com/career-advice/career-development/assertiveness-skills

Author talks: Kristin Neff on harnessing fierce self-compassion. (2021, June 15). McKinsey & Company. https://www.mckinsey.com/featured-insights/mckinsey-on-books/author-talks-kristin-neff-on-harnessing-fierce-self-compassion

Bagnall, B. (2016, June 27). *5 ways to stay motivated when you experience setbacks*. HuffPost. https://www.huffpost.

com/entry/5-ways-to-stay-
motivated_b_10664424/amp

Barca, M. (2023). *Understanding the 'social' in social
anxiety.* Pursuit. https://pursuit.unimelb.edu.au/arti
cles/understanding-the-social-in-social-anxiety.amp

Barnett, M., Maciel, I. V., Johnson, D., & Ciepluch, I.
(2021). Social anxiety and perceived social support:
Gender differences and the mediating role of communication styles. *Psychological Reports, 124*(1), 70–87.
https://doi.org/10.1177/0033294119900975

Batterham, A. (2021, December 14). *How to be your own
cheerleader.* Medium. https://audrey-batterham.
medium.com/how-to-be-your-own-cheerleader-
a68657726329

Begonia, C. (2023, May 9). *The psychology of impostor
syndrome & how to actually overcome it.* Mindbodygreen.
https://www.mindbodygreen.com/articles/imposter-
syndrome

Being assertive: Reduce stress, communicate better. (2022,
May 13). Mayo Clinic. https://www.mayoclinic.org/
healthy-lifestyle/stress-management/in-depth/
assertive/art-20044644

Bjornsson, A. S., Hardarson, J. P., Valdimarsdottir, A. G.,
Gudmundsdottir, K., Tryggvadottir, A., Thorarinsdot-

tir, K., Wessman, I., Sigurjónsdóttir, Ó., Davidsdottir, S., & Thorisdottir, A. (2020). Social trauma and its association with posttraumatic stress disorder and social anxiety disorder. *Journal of Anxiety Disorders, 72,* 102228. https://doi.org/10.1016/j.janxdis.2020.102228

Boardman, S. (2022, April 25). *How to push past fear.* Positive Prescription. https://positiveprescription.com/push-past-fear/

Brazier, Y. (2020, November 27). *Everything you need to know about phobias.* Medical News Today. https://www.medicalnewstoday.com/articles/249347#causes

Brower, T. (2022, July 4). *Follow your passion really is good advice: 3 ways to fuel your career.* Forbes. https://www.forbes.com/sites/tracybrower/2022/07/04/follow-your-passion-really-is-good-advice-3-ways-to-fuel-your-career/?sh=7aa89dcc2cdd

Brumariu, L. E., & Kerns, K. A. (2008). Mother–child attachment and social anxiety symptoms in middle childhood. *Journal of Applied Developmental Psychology, 29*(5), 393–402. https://doi.org/10.1016/j.appdev.2008.06.002

Building and maintaining healthy relationships. (n.d.). Healthdirect. https://www.healthdirect.gov.au/amp/article/building-and-maintaining-healthy-relationships

Causes of Social Anxiety. (2020, October 9). Bridges to Recovery. https://www.bridgestorecovery.com/social-anxiety/causes-social-anxiety/amp/#9-social-anxiety-triggers

Causes of stress: Recognizing and managing your stressors. (2020, March 29). Healthline. https://www.healthline.com/health/stress-causes

CBT STRATEGIES TO OVERCOME SOCIAL ANXIETY. (2021, September 24). National Social Anxiety Center. https://nationalsocialanxietycenter.com/cognitive-behavioral-therapy/social-anxiety-strategies/

Celestine, N. (2021). *How to improve communication skills: 14 best worksheets.* Positive Psychology. https://positivepsychology.com/how-to-improve-communication-skills/#games

Choosing Therapy, & Arzt, N. (2023). *Shyness vs. Social anxiety: Understanding the difference.* Choosing Therapy. https://www.choosingtherapy.com/social-anxiety-vs-shyness/#:~:text=Shyness%20can%20turn%20into%20social,patterns%20can%20trigger%20anxiety%20symptoms.

Chowdhury, M. R. (2023). *Emotional regulation: 6 key skills to regulate emotions.* Positive Psychology. https://positivepsychology.com/emotion-regulation/

Cohut, M. (2019, August 30). *4 top tips for coping with social anxiety*. Medical News Today. https://www.medicalnewstoday.com/articles/326211#4.-Do-some thing-nice-for-someone

Cooks-Campbell, A. (2022, May 16). Pandemic awkwardness holding you back? 10 tips to rediscover your social self. *BetterUp Blog*. https://www.betterup.com/blog/how-to-improve-social-skills?hs_amp=true

Coultas, I. (2018, August 13). *Measure social competence with the social skills inventory*. Mind Garden. https://www.mindgarden.com/blog/post/40-measure-social-competence-with-the-social-skills-inventory

Cuncic, A. (2018). *Reduce your social anxiety with these 20 journal prompts*. About Social Anxiety. https://www.aboutsocialanxiety.com/anxiety-journal-prompts/

Cuncic, A. (2020a). *Avoidance behaviors and social anxiety disorder*. Verywell Mind. https://www.verywellmind.com/what-are-avoidance-behaviors-3024312

Cuncic, A. (2020b). *Avoidance behaviors and social anxiety disorder*. Verywell Mind. https://www.verywellmind.com/effect-of-hormones-on-social-anxiety-4129255#:~:text=Chang-ing%20levels%20of%20the%20-sex,be%20linked%20to%20anxiety%20symptoms.

Cuncic, A. (2020c). *An overview of social skills training.* *Verywell Mind.* https://www.verywellmind.com/social-skills-4157216

Cuncic, A. (2020d). *Differences between shyness and social anxiety disorder.* Verywell Mind. https://www.verywell mind.com/difference-between-shyness-and-social-anxiety-disorder-3024431

Cuncic, A. (2021a). *Understanding the causes of social anxiety disorder.* Verywell Mind. https://www.verywell mind.com/social-anxiety-disorder-causes-3024749#:

Cuncic, A. (2021b). *Anxiety disorder relaxation techniques.* Verywell Mind. https://www.verywellmind.com/relax ation-techniques-for-sad-3024334

Cuncic, A. (2021c, September 1). *Therapy for social anxiety disorder.* Verywell Mind. https://www.verywell mind.com/how-is-cbt-used-to-treat-sad-3024945

Cuncic, A. (2022a). *How do I practice mindfulness medita-tion for social anxiety disorder?* Verywell Mind. https://www.verywellmind.com/meditation-for-social-anxi ety-3024211#citation-2

Cuncic, A. (2022b). *What is active listening?* Verywell Mind. https://www.verywellmind.com/what-is-active-listening-3024343

Cuncic, A. (2023). *Negative thoughts: How to stop them.* Verywell Mind. https://www.verywellmind.com/how-to-change-negative-thinking-3024843

Cuncic, A., MA. (2020e). *How to practice exposure therapy for social anxiety disorder.* Verywell Mind. https://www.verywellmind.com/practice-social-anxiety-disorder-exposure-therapy-3024845

Darcin, A. E., Kose, S., Noyan, C. O., Nurmedov, S., Yilmaz, O., & Dilbaz, N. (2016). Smartphone addiction and its relationship with social anxiety and loneliness. *Behaviour & Information Technology, 35*(7), 520–525. https://doi.org/10.1080/0144929x.2016.1158319

DBT emotion regulation skills (Worksheet). (n.d.). Therapist Aid. https://www.therapistaid.com/therapy-work sheet/dbt-emotion-regulation-skills

Dempsey, K. (2019, January 13). *How to spot someone with social anxiety disorder.* The Awareness Centre. https://theawarenesscentre.com/how-to-spot-some one-with-social-anxiety-disorder/

Deupree, S. (2023). *CBT for social anxiety: How it works, examples & effectiveness.* Choosing Therapy. https://www.choosingtherapy.com/cbt-for-social-anxiety/#:~:text=Relaxation%20exercis-es%20are%20another%20important,therapeutic%20ap-proaches%20like%20exposure%20therapy.

Developing Your Support System. (2023, February 21). University at Buffalo School of Social Work - University at Buffalo. https://socialwork.buffalo.edu/resources/self-care-starter-kit/additional-self-care-resources/developing-your-support-system.html

Dibdin, E. (2021, July 2). *How meditation can help you manage social anxiety.* Psych Central. https://psychcentral.com/anxiety/how-meditation-can-help-you-manage-social-anxiety#effectiveness

Dragan, M., & Dragan, W. Ł. (2014). Temperament and anxiety: The mediating role of metacognition. *Journal of Psychopathology and Behavioral Assessment, 36*(2), 246–254. https://doi.org/10.1007/s10862-013-9392-z

11 healthy ways to handle life's stressors. (2022, October 21). American Psychological Association. https://www.apa.org/topics/stress/tips

Facing your fears exercise. (n.d.). Think CBT. https://thinkcbt.com/facing-your-fears-exercise

Falloon, I. R., Lloyd, G. G., & Harpin, R. E. (1981). The treatment of social phobia. *Journal of Nervous and Mental Disease, 169*(3), 180–184. https://doi.org/10.1097/00005053-198103000-00005

Felman, A. (2023a, February 2). *What to know about anxiety.* Medical News Today. https://www.medical newstoday.com/articles/323454

Felman, A. (2023b, May 25). *What to know about social anxiety disorder.* Medical News Today. https://www. medicalnewstoday.com/articles/176891

Feyoh, M. (2023). *29 journaling prompts for anxiety help in 2023.* Happier Human. https://www.happierhuman. com/journaling-prompts-anxiety/

Fingerman, K. L. (2020, September 25). *Use of technologies for social connectedness and well-being and as a tool for research data collection in older adults.* Mobile Technology for Adaptive Aging - NCBI Bookshelf. https://www. ncbi.nlm.nih.gov/books/NBK563112/

Fritscher, L. (2023). *The psychology of fear.* Verywell Mind. https://www.verywellmind.com/the-psychol ogy-of-fear-2671696

Gallagher, D. (2021). *The self-care routine that helps with my social anxiety.* Spunout. https://spunout.ie/voices/ advice/self-care-routine-help-social-anxiety

Gilbertson, T. (2013, October 19). Self-Esteem vs. Self-Criticism. *GoodTherapy.org Therapy Blog.* https://www. goodtherapy.org/blog/self-esteem-vs-self-criticism/

Goldin, P. R., Ramel, W., & Gross, J. J. (2009). Mindfulness meditation training and self-referential processing in social anxiety disorder: Behavioral and neural effects. *Journal of Cognitive Psychotherapy, 23*(3), 242–257. https://doi.org/10.1891/0889-8391.23.3.242

Greenberg, D., Warrier, V., Abu-Akel, A., Allison, C., Gajos, K. Z., Reinecke, K., Rentfrow, P. J., Radecki, M. A., & Baron-Cohen, S. (2022). Sex and age differences in "theory of mind" across 57 countries using the english version of the "reading the mind in the eyes" test. *Proceedings of the National Academy of Sciences of the United States of America, 120*(1). https://doi.org/10.1073/pnas.2022385119

Greene, P. (2022, June 26). *Avoidance: There's no escaping its importance to anxiety.* Manhattan Center for Cognitive Behavioral Therapy. https://www.manhattancbt.com/archives/785/avoidance/

Griffin, T. (2022). *6 ways to recognize social anxiety disorder.* wikiHow. https://www.wikihow.com/Recognize-Social-Anxiety-Disorder

Gunn, D. (2022). 10 most valuable networking skills for every professional. *CodeinWP.* https://www.codeinwp.com/blog/networking-skills/#gref

Gunzelmann, A. (2022, August 17). *Why we need fierce self-compassion for women.* Tbd.Community. https://

www.tbd.community/en/a/why-we-need-fierce-self-compassion-women

Harmer, S. (2023). *Why a happy and successful life is more than just money*. Lifehack. https://www.lifehack.org/arti cles/money/10-reasons-why-following-your-passion-more-important-than-money.html

Harvard Health. (2020, August 1). *Recognizing and easing the physical symptoms of anxiety*. Harvard Health Publishing. https://www.health.harvard.edu/mind-and-mood/recognizing-and-easing-the-physical-symp toms-of-anxiety

Heiser, N., Turner, S. M., Beidel, D. C., & Roberson-Nay, R. (2009). Differentiating social phobia from shyness. *Journal of Anxiety Disorders, 23*(4), 469–476. https://doi.org/10.1016/j.janxdis.2008.10.002

Herrity, J. (2023). *10 ways to develop and improve your social skills*. Indeed. https://www.indeed.com/career-advice/career-development/developing-social-skills

Horton, C. (2023). *13 confidence building exercises every woman needs to try*. Clever Girl Finance. https://www.clevergirlfinance.com/confidence-building-exercises/

How to be an effective communicator in 7 easy steps. (2022, November 8). Walden University. https://www.waldenu.edu/programs/communication/resource/

how-to-be-an-effective-communicator-in-7-easy-steps

How to become an effective communicator. (2023b). Indeed. https://www.indeed.com/career-advice/career-development/effective-communicator

How to become more confident in 8 powerful ways. (2022b). Indeed. https://www.indeed.com/career-advice/career-development/how-to-become-more-confident

How to build and maintain a social support network. (2021). Hopeful Panda. https://hopefulpanda.com/social-support-network/

How to deal with panic attacks. (n.d.). NHS Inform. https://www.nhsinform.scot/healthy-living/mental-wellbeing/anxiety-and-panic/how-to-deal-with-panic-attacks

How to manage anxiety and fear. (n.d.). Mental Health Foundation. https://www.mentalhealth.org.uk/explore-mental-health/publications/how-overcome-anxiety-and-fear

Johansson, M. (2020, August 3). *Returning to society and the rise of social anxiety.* Well Clinic. https://wellsanfrancisco.com/returning-to-society-and-the-rise-of-social-anxiety/

Johnson, D., & Whisman, M. A. (2013). Gender differences in rumination: A meta-analysis. *Personality and Individual Differences, 55*(4), 367–374. https://doi.org/10.1016/j.paid.2013.03.019

Johnson, E. B. (2019, July 12). *Challenge your negative thoughts and improve the quality of your life.* Medium. https://medium.com/practical-growth/challenge-your-negative-thoughts-275e05159e67

Khan, M. A., & Khan, N. (2020). Effects of psychosocial and socio-environmental factors on anxiety disorder among adolescents in Bangladesh. *Brain and Behavior, 10*(12). https://doi.org/10.1002/brb3.1899

Konkel, L. (2023, April 25). *What is anxiety? Symptoms, causes, diagnosis, treatment, and prevention.* Everyday Health. https://www.everydayhealth.com/anxiety/guide/

Kopetz, C., Woerner, J., & Briskin, J. L. (2018). Another look at impulsivity: Could impulsive behavior be strategic? *Social and Personality Psychology Compass, 12*(5), e12385. https://doi.org/10.1111/spc3.12385

Koutsky, J. (2023, February 22). *Wondering why some women seem so effortlessly confident? We uncovered 23 of their best-kept secrets.* Parade: Entertainment, Recipes, Health, Life, Holidays. https://parade.com/1229840/judykoutsky/confident-woman/

KPMG study finds 75% of executive women experience imposter syndrome. (2020, October 27). KPMG. https://info.kpmg.us/news-perspectives/people-culture/kpmg-study-finds-most-female-executives-experience-imposter-syndrome.html

Kurtuy, A. (2023). 11+top networking skills you must have in 2023. *Novorésumé.* https://novoresume.com/career-blog/networking-skills/amp

Lancer, D. (2020). *Self-criticism – self-esteem's saboteur.* What Is Codependency? https://whatiscodependency.com/self-criticism-self-esteem-raising-selfesteem/

Lancia, G. (2023). *Social skills training for adults: 10 best activities + PDF.* Positive Psychology. https://positivepsychology.com/social-skills-training/#activities

Leigh, E., & Clark, D. (2018).Understanding social anxiety disorder in adolescents and improving treatment outcomes: Applying the cognitive model of Clark and wells (1995). *Clinical Child and Family Psychology Review, 21*(3), 388–414. https://doi.org/10.1007/s10567-018-0258-5

Lid, W. (2023, March 14). *Strategies for overcoming obstacles and setbacks.* Medium. https://medium.com/@walid_9453/strategies-for-overcoming-obstacles-and-setbacks-c819b3a902fc

Linsey. (2022, January 17). *10 insightful journal prompts for social anxiety*. Annais. https://annais.co.uk/journal-prompts-for-social-anxiety/

Lovering, N. (2022, August 17). *The link between PTSD and social anxiety*. Psych Central. https://psychcentral.com/ptsd/childhood-trauma-social-anxiety

LpcRice, M. (2022). *Cognitive behavioral therapy (CBT) For social anxiety*. Talkspace. https://www.talkspace.com/blog/cbt-for-social-anxiety/

MacCutcheon, M. (2018, August 29). Women and self-worth: 5 steps to improving self-esteem. *GoodTherapy.org Therapy Blog*. https://www.goodtherapy.org/blog/women-and-self-worth-5-steps-to-improving-self-esteem-0829184/amp/

Magazine, C. (2022, April 28). *Doctor explains how women can overcome imposter syndrome*. The CEO Magazine. https://www.theceomagazine.com/opinion/women-imposter-syndrome/#:

Marston-Salem, N. (2020). *Why do women struggle more with anxiety?* Fountain Hills Recovery. https://fountainhillsrecovery.com/blog/why-women-struggle-with-anxiety/#:

Martins, J. (2022, October 27). *How to practice active listening (With examples)*. Asana. https://asana.com/resources/active-listening

Masi, Y. (2021, December 7). *6 ways to push past fear into your purpose*. Medium. https://medium.datadrivenin vestor.com/6-ways-to-push-past-fear-into-your-purpose-f58a8762755e

Mastering conversation: The art of small talk. (n.d.). UniversalClass.com. https://www.universalclass.com/articles/self-help/mastering-conversation-the-art-of-small-talk.htm

McIntosh, J. (2023, April 21). *What you need to know about agoraphobia*. Medical News Today. https://www.medicalnewstoday.com/articles/162169#treatment

McMillan, K. A., Sareen, J., & Asmundson, G. J. (2014). Social anxiety disorder is associated with ptsd symptom presentation: An exploratory study within a nationally representative sample. *Journal of Traumatic Stress, 27*(5), 602–609. https://doi.org/10.1002/jts.21952

Meadows, M. (2021). *How to be your own cheerleader in life!* The Positive Planners. https://www.thepositive planners.com/how-to-be-your-own-cheerleader-in-life/

Menzies, F. (2019). Developing Self-Confidence for Women. *Include-Empower.Com.* https://culturepluscon sulting.com/2018/04/28/developing-self-confidence-for-women/?amp=1

Miker, S. (2022, March 19). *4 reasons following your passion leads to success.* Entrepreneur. https://www. entrepreneur.com/leadership/4-reasons-following-your-passion-leads-to-success/419610

Millacci, T. S. (2020). *How to relax: Best relaxation techniques for anxiety.* Positive Psychology. https://posi tivepsychology.com/relaxation-techniques-anxiety/

Mitchell, J. (n.d.). *Technology and social connection.* Pressbooks. https://uen.pressbooks.pub/tech1010/chapter/technology-and-social-connection/

Monae, A. (2023, January 31). *Here's why you should stop expecting support from others and become your own cheerleader.* Entrepreneur. https://www.entrepreneur.com/living/why-you-need-to-become-your-own-cheer leader/442979

Morales, S. C., Brown, K. M., Taber-Thomas, B. C., LoBue, V., Buss, K. A., & Pérez-Edgar, K. (2017). Maternal anxiety predicts attentional bias towards threat in infancy. *Emotion, 17*(5), 874–883. https://doi.org/10.1037/emo0000275

Nall, R. (2023a, February 10). *What is separation anxiety disorder in adults?* Medical News Today. https://www.medicalnewstoday.com/articles/322070#causes-in-adults

Nall, R. (2023b, May 24). *What to know about panic attacks and panic disorder.* Medical News Today. https://www.medicalnewstoday.com/articles/8872#risk-factors

Nash, J. (2020). *Building healthy relationships with 40 helpful worksheets.* Positive Psychology. https://positivepsychology.com/healthy-relationships-worksheets/#adults

Neff, K. (2018, October 9). *Why women need fierce self-compassion.* Self-Compassion. https://self-compassion.org/women-fierce-self-compassion/

Norton, A., & Abbott, M. J. (2017). The role of environmental factors in the aetiology of social anxiety disorder: A review of the theoretical and empirical literature. *Behaviour Change, 34*(2), 76–97. https://doi.org/10.1017/bec.2017.7

Nunez, K. (2020, June 9). *5 benefits of metta meditation and how to do it.* Healthline. https://www.healthline.com/health/metta-meditation

Onumaegbu, P. (2023, March 27). *Persistence: 11 strategies for staying motivated and persistent in the face of challenges and setbacks &ra . . .Pawns: Grow, Level, Step Up.* https://pawns.com.ng/persistence/

Overview - Cognitive behavioural therapy (CBT). (n.d.). nhs.uk. https://www.nhs.uk/mental-health/talking-therapies-medicine-treatments/talking-therapies-and-counselling/cognitive-behavioural-therapy-cbt/overview/#:

Perry, E. (2023, March 24). Self-esteem isn't everything, but these 5 tips can give you a boost. *BetterUp Blog.* https://www.betterup.com/blog/how-to-improve-self-esteem?hs_amp=true

Priyamvada, R., Kumari, S., Prakash, J., & Chaudhury, S. (2009). Cognitive behavioral therapy in the treatment of social phobia. *Industrial Psychiatry Journal, 18*(1), 60. https://doi.org/10.4103/0972-6748.57863

Quinn, D. (2023). *Cognitive restructuring in cbt: Steps, techniques, & examples.* Sandstone Care. https://www.sandstonecare.com/blog/cognitive-restructuring-cbt/

Rastogi, S. (2022, October 31). *Imposter syndrome affects women more than men.* HerZindagi English. https://www.herzindagi.com/society-culture/imposter-syndrome-affects-more-women-than-men-article-212427#:~:text=Imposter%20Syndrome%20is%20de-

fined%20as,normal%20and%20what%20is%20de-
served.%E2%80%9D

Rauch, J. (2017). What causes social anxiety? *Talkspace*.
https://www.talkspace.com/blog/what-causes-social-
anxiety/#2

Raypole, C. (2021, September 17). *How CBT can help you
manage social anxiety symptoms*. Healthline. https://
www.healthline.com/health/anxiety/social-anxiety-
disorder-cognitive-behavioral-therapy#how-it-works

Raypole, C. (2023a, March 10). *Cognitive behavioral therapy: What is it and how does it work?* Healthline. https://
www.healthline.com/health/cognitive-behavioral-
therapy#techniques

Raypole, C. (2023b, March 29). *Physical symptoms of
anxiety: How does it feel?* Healthline. https://www.health
line.com/health/physical-symptoms-of-
anxiety#treatment

Remes, O., Brayne, C., Van Der Linde, R. M., & Lafor-
tune, L. (2016). A systematic review of reviews on the
prevalence of anxiety disorders in adult populations.
Brain and Behavior, 6(7), e00497. https://doi.org/10.
1002/brb3.497

Roncero, A. (2021, June 21). Automatic negative
thoughts: how to identify and fix them. *BetterUpBlog*.

https://www.betterup.com/blog/automatic-thoughts?
hs_amp=true

Roth, D. A., & Gross, J. J. (2001). COGNATIVE-
BEHAVIORAL MODELS OF SOCIAL ANXIETY
DISORDER. *Psychiatric Clinics of North America, 24*(4),
753–771.   https://doi.org/10.1016/s0193-
953x(05)70261-6

Rudaz, M., Ledermann, T., Margraf, J., Becker, E. S., &
Craske, M. G. (2017). The moderating role of avoidance
behavior on anxiety over time: Is there a difference
between social anxiety disorder and specific phobia?
PLOS ONE, 12(7), e0180298. https://doi.org/10.1371/
journal.pone.0180298

Sangperm, N., Sangperm, W., & Aramrueang, P. (2020,
July 1). Role of self-motivation and social skills in
performance. *Elselvier.* https://papers.ssrn.com/sol3/
papers.cfm?abstract_id=3888075

Saxena, S. (2022). *Avoidance behavior: Examples, impacts,
& how to overcome.* Choosing Therapy. https://www.
choosingtherapy.com/avoidance-behavior/

Schaffner, A. K. (2020). *How to practice self-care: 10+
worksheets and 12 ideas.* Positive Psychology. https://posi
tivepsychology.com/self-care-worksheets/#wheel

Scheurich, J. A., Beidel, D. C., & Vanryckeghem, M. (2019). Exposure therapy for social anxiety disorder in people who stutter: An exploratory multiple baseline design. *Journal of Fluency Disorders, 59*, 21–32. https://doi.org/10.1016/j.jfludis.2018.12.001

Segrin, C., & Kinney, T. A. (1995). Social skills deficits among the socially anxious: Rejection from others and loneliness. *Motivation and Emotion, 19*(1), 1–24. https://doi.org/10.1007/bf02260670

Self-esteem self-help resources - Information sheets & workbooks. (n.d.). Centre for Clinical Interventions. https://www.cci.health.wa.gov.au/Resources/Looking-After-Yourself/Self-Esteem

Shortsleeve, C. (2023, January 5). *How to practice self-compassion and build a stable sense of confidence*. Women's Health. https://www.womenshealthmag.com/health/a42156653/self-compassion-how-to-be-more-confident/

SOCIAL ANXIETY DISORDER. (2013). British Psychological Association. https://www.ncbi.nlm.nih.gov/books/NBK327674/#:~:text=Individuals%20with%20social%20anxiety%20disorder,feared%20outcomes)%20can%20vary%20independently.

Social skills training: Definition, uses and types. (2022a). Indeed. https://in.indeed.com/career-advice/career-development/social-skills-training

6 major types of anxiety disorders. (2019). CHOC - Children's Health Hub. https://health.choc.org/6-major-types-of-anxiety-disorders/

6 tips to relax in social situations. (2018). Counselling Directory. https://www.counselling-directory.org.uk/memberarticles/feeling-overwhelmed-in-social-situa tions-6-tips-to-calm-your-social-anxiety

Smith, J. (2023, April 14). *How can you stop a panic attack?* Medical News Today. https://www.medicalnew stoday.com/articles/321510

Social anxiety disorder. (n.d.). National Institute of Mental Health (NIMH). https://www.nimh.nih.gov/health/statistics/social-anxiety-disorder

Social anxiety disorder: More than just shyness. (n.d.). National Institute of Mental Health (NIMH). https://www.nimh.nih.gov/health/publications/social-anxiety-disorder-more-than-just-shyness#:~:text=A%20person%20with%20social%20anxiety,a%20cashier%20in%20a%20store.

Social anxiety disorder (social phobia) - Symptoms and causes. (2021, June 19). Mayo Clinic. https://www.mayoclinic.org/diseases-conditions/social-anxiety-disorder/symptoms-causes/syc-20353561#:

Social anxiety is highly heritable but is affected by environment. (2016, January 16). ScienceDaily. https://www.sciencedaily.com/releases/2016/01/160120092655.htm

Social anxiety self-help resources - Information sheets & workbooks. (n.d.). Centre for Clinical Interventions. https://www.cci.health.wa.gov.au/Resources/Looking-After-Yourself/Social-Anxiety

Stanborough, R. J. (2020, February 4). *How to change negative thinking with cognitive restructuring.* Healthline. https://www.healthline.com/health/cognitive-restructuring#drawbacks

Stangier, U., Schramm, E., Heidenreich, T., Berger, M., & Clark, D. (2011). Cognitive therapy vs interpersonal psychotherapy in social anxiety disorder. *Archives of General Psychiatry, 68*(7), 692. https://doi.org/10.1001/archgenpsychiatry.2011.67

Stress: Coping with life's stressors. (n.d.). Cleveland Clinic. https://my.clevelandclinic.org/health/articles/6392-stress-coping-with-lifes-stressors

Strong, P. (2011, January 26). *Overcoming social anxiety with mindfulness therapy.* MentalHelp.net. https://www.mentalhelp.net/blogs/overcoming-social-anxiety-with-mindfulness-therapy/

Sutton, J. (2023a). *Role play in therapy: 21 scripts & examples for your session.* Positive Psychology. https://positivepsychology.com/role-playing-scripts/

Sutton, J. (2023b). *18 anxiety worksheets for adults, teens & more.* Positive Psychology. https://positivepsychology.com/anxiety-worksheets/#3-social-anxiety-worksheets

10 common negative thinking patterns and 5 steps for change. (2023, June 1). The Family Centre. https://www.familycentre.org/news/post/10-common-negative-thinking-patterns-and-5-steps-for-change

10 top steps on how to overcome fear and achieve goals. (2023, May 19). tonyrobbins.com. https://www.tonyrobbins.com/stories/unleash-the-power/overcoming-fear-in-5-steps/

The female "soft skills" that can boost workplace success. (2020, March 8). Goodnet. https://www.goodnet.org/articles/female-soft-skills-that-boost-workplace-success

The importance of effective communication. (n.d.). Stevenson University. https://www.stevenson.edu/online/about-us/news/importance-effective-communication/#:

The 7 benefits of effective communication in personal and professional settings. (2019, July 19). Portland Community College. https://climb.pcc.edu/blog/the-7-bene fits-of-effective-communication-in-personal-and-professional-settings

Thurnell-Read, J. (2020). *How to cope with difficult social situations.* Thrive Global. https://community.thriveg lobal.com/how-to-cope-with-difficult-social-situations/

The art of small talk. (n.d.). Toastmasters International. https://www.toastmasters.org/magazine/articles/the-art-of-small-talk

Top tips on building and maintaining healthy relationships. (n.d.). Mental Health Foundation. https://www.mental health.org.uk/our-work/public-engagement/healthy-relationships/top-tips-building-and-maintaining-healthy-relationships

Tull, M. (2020). *The relationship between PTSD and social anxiety disorder.* Verywell Mind. https://www.verywell mind.com/ptsd-and-social-anxiety-disorder-2797528

Types of anxiety. (n.d.). Beyond Blue. https://www. beyondblue.org.au/mental-health/anxiety/types-of-anxiety

Vaghefi, I., Lapointe, L., & Boudreau-Pinsonneault, C. (2017). A typology of user liability to IT addiction. *Information Systems Journal, 27*(2), 125–169. https://doi. org/10.1111/isj.12098

Villines, Z. (2021, September 28). *Selective mutism in adults and children.* Medical News Today. https://www. medicalnewstoday.com/articles/selective-mutism#causes

Villines, Z. (2022, June 20). *Cognitive restructuring and its techniques.* Medical News Today. https://www.medical newstoday.com/articles/cognitive-restructuring#benefits

Walinga, J. (2014, October 17). *16.2 Stress and coping.* Pressbooks. https://opentextbc.ca/introductiontopsy chology/chapter/15-2-stress-and-coping/

Weiss, R. (2022). *Why am I afraid to say "no"? Social anxiety and the lack of assertiveness.* National Social Anxiety Center. https://nationalsocialanxietycenter. com/2022/02/21/why-am-i-afraid-to-say-no-social-anxiety-and-the-lack-of-assertiveness/

What are the signs and symptoms of social anxiety? (2020, October 9). Bridges to Recovery. https://www. bridgestorecovery.com/social-anxiety/signs-symp toms-social-anxiety/amp/#5-physiological-symptoms-of-social-anxiety-disorder

What is cognitive behavioral therapy? (2017, July 31). American Psychological Association. https://www.apa.org/ptsd-guideline/patients-and-families/cognitive-behavioral

What is exposure therapy? (2017, July 31). American Psychological Association. https://www.apa.org/ptsd-guideline/patients-and-families/exposure-therapy#:~:text=In%20this%20form%20of%20therapy,reduce%20fear%20and%20decrease%20avoidance.

What is fear? | What causes fear? (2021, November 13). Paul Ekman Group. https://www.paulekman.com/universal-emotions/what-is-fear/

Why social anxiety disorder is more and more common in our society. (2020). Resources to Recover. https://www.rtor.org/2020/01/29/why-social-anxiety-disorder-is-common-in-our-society/#:~:text=All%20people%20feel%20uncomfortable%20in,more%20common%20in%20everyday%20society.

Wiebe, J. (2019, August 9). *What is the relationship between hormones and anxiety?* Talkspace. https://www.talkspace.com/mental-health/conditions/articles/anxiety-hormones-connection/

Wooll, M. (2022, February 7). Overcome self-criticism by getting your inner critic to take a break. *BetterUp*

Blog. https://www.betterup.com/blog/self-criticism? hs_amp=true

Xu, Y., Schneier, F. R., Gross, J. J., Princisvalle, K., Liebowitz, M. R., Wang, S., & Blanco, C. (2012). Gender differences in social anxiety disorder: Results from the national epidemiologic sample on alcohol and related conditions. *Journal of Anxiety Disorders, 26*(1), 12–19. https://doi.org/10.1016/j.janxdis.2011.08.006

Yasmin, N. (2022). *50 social anxiety quotes that Will alleviate your anxiety at work. Vantage Fit.* https://www. vantagefit.io/blog/social-anxiety-quotes/

Yetman, D. (2021, June 21). *Exposure therapy.* Healthline. https://www.healthline.com/health/exposure-therapy

Made in the USA
Las Vegas, NV
10 January 2024

84161065R10118